A Time for My Singing

A Time for My Singing

Witness of a Life

Nalini Marcia Jayasuriya

with an introduction by
John W. Cook

OMSC Publications
New Haven, Connecticut USA
www.OMSC.org

A Time for My Singing
Witness of a Life

First published December 2004

© OMSC Publications, 2004

Published by
Overseas Ministries Study Center
490 Prospect Street
New Haven, CT 06511 USA
(203) 624-6672
www.OMSC.org

ISBN: 0-9762205-0-4

Cataloguing-in-publication data is available from the Library of Congress.

Design: Daniel J. Nicholas

Printed in China

in the emptiness of my desert
your voice brings new flowers
in the darkness of my night
you circle a star;
remembering your words
your presence
is Now

can you believe
can you understand
can you ever measure the power of my faith
that has gathered your flowers
and circled your stars
to the place of my heart?

I Simurgh, Bird of the Diamond Face
Storm-footed, quivering on fire-spun wings
eye of the sun
fire of the sea
spell of all dreaming unuttered things:
I Simurgh, Bird of the Diamond Face
heart of the Sky
circle of Time, of infinite Space—
Remember; speak without fear
Think; think only of Me
and I am ten thousand birds—
Touch me
And I disappear . . .

Contents

Part II Reminiscences

The Artist

An internationally known artist from Sri Lanka, Nalini M. Jayasuriya has exhibited her soul-stirring paintings in Manila, London, Bangkok, Paris, Toronto, Tokyo, Jerusalem, and New York, and has lectured at universities around the world, including Yale Divinity School, New Haven, Connecticut, and Tokyo University, Tokyo, Japan. She was Artist in Residence for two years at the Overseas Ministries Study Center, New Haven. A Christian since age seven, Jayasuriya was raised in Sri Lanka by Anglican parents.

Nalini was awarded Sri Lanka's highest honour for the Arts by the President of Sri Lanka, Her Excellency, Chandrika Bandaranaike Kumaratunga. The title is Kala Keerthi.

Nalini Jayasuriya's previous works include two volumes of her paintings and text published in Japanese with the aid of Dr. Yoshiko Ishikki and Professor Masao Takenaka. Nalini's books published in Sri Lanka are *Cargo*, a book of poems; *Letters from Ingy*, letters from her cat; and *When Jesus Was Born*.

Nalini Jayasuriya

* * * *

I come from a land of rich, ancient, and diverse cultures and traditions. While I carry the enriching influences of both West and East, I express myself through an Asian and Christian consciousness with respect for all confessions of religious faith.

This book is for many, in many countries I have been in and whom I have been privileged to know. I am deeply grateful to my gifted parents, to my very gifted only brother, and to many others who are not named here, but who have enriched my life with their faithful care and wisdom, and the help always given me, often unasked for. Some of these faithful people are those we still call servants in Sri Lanka, and two of the best have been my old ayah and dear old Appuhamy, my man Friday, who never said he could not do what I asked him to do but always suggested another way; and I admit, his way was always better!

Nalini Jayasuriya
Overseas Ministries Study Center
New Haven, Connecticut
March 18, 2003

Preface

I am pleased to present this inaugural volume of an anticipated annual series featuring the work of outstanding Asian artists who have spent an academic sabbatical year at the Overseas Ministries Study Center in New Haven. That the premiere offering in this series should be *by* and *about* world-renowned Sri Lankan artist, Ms. Nalini Jayasuriya, is particularly gratifying. Nalini was the Paul Lauby Artist in Residence at the Overseas Ministries Study Center from October of 2001 through March of 2003. Painting, exhibiting, writing, and lecturing during her time at the center—this volume represents no more than a tithe of her remarkable creativity and industry.

Nalini's many friends and admirers know that her life is as colorful and as variegated as her art. The sheer range of her professional repertoire—teacher, broadcaster, writer, musician, art director, painter, sculptor, and potter, as proficient with stained glass and enamel as she is with pen and brush—hints at the multifarious talents and boundless energies with which she has been endowed, and which she has so generously bequested to students, colleagues and admirers around the world.

She has taught and lectured at eminent universities and other centers of learning in Sweden, Denmark, Switzerland, the United Kingdom, Israel, and the United States. As Elizabeth Luce Moore Professor, she taught courses for graduating seniors at universities in the Philippines, Japan, Thailand, and Pakistan.

Numerous books of art in several languages have featured her work, and her painting, sculpture, pottery, stained glass, and enamels have been exhibited in London, Cambridge, Chelmsford, Bonn, Cologne, Stuttgart, Paris, St. Dizier, Zurich, Copenhagen, Rattvik, Vancouver, New York, Washington D.C., Louisville, and New Haven, as well as in Japan, Israel, Philippines, Indonesia, and Malaysia. And in Sri Lanka over the years, her exhibitions and lectures have been sponsored not only by the cultural institutions of Sri Lanka itself, but also by the cultural departments of the British High Commission, the Republic of India, and the embassies of the United States, France, Germany, and Israel.

Images—on screen and video, in magazines and newspapers, on billboards and posters—are ubiquitous, inescapable, and powerful shapers of our modern perceptions of both what *is* and what *should be*. The skillful manipulation of images can sway opinion, perpetrate stereotypes, and distort reality, peddling everything from peace to pandemonium. Echoing the eccentric but prescient William Blake, we humans are prone to embrace a lie when we see *with*, rather than *through*, the eye. By means of a single image, etching itself permanently in a viewer's consciousness, truth is verified, subverted, or dismissed.

In an age when our cultural image makers manifest an almost pathological pre-occupation with the terrible, the dysfunctional, and the tragic, relying as they do for their very livelihood on the human fascination with shocking spectacle, Nalini offers us, through her art, the gift of peace. Her paintings help us to see *through* the eye. Simple, yet profound; direct, yet subtle; evocative, yet uncluttered; serene, yet dynamic: her art offers those with eyes to see color without garishness, spirituality without vacuity, invitation without coercion.

The pristine simplicity and flowing congruity of her art resonates with our own sometimes sadly latent spirituality—fostering within us a wistful longing for that which is deepest and best in our nature. Nalini's work serves as an eloquent and compelling exposition of some well-known but rarely followed counsel offered nearly 2000 years ago by St. Paul:

> *Whatever is true, whatever is honorable, whatever is just, whatever is pure, whatever is pleasing, whatever is commendable, if there is any excellence and if there is anything worthy of praise, think about these things . . . and the God of peace will be with you.* (Philippians 4:8–9 NRSV)

It is appropriate that Paul Lauby, in whose honor the artist-in-residence fellowships are named, and who played such a vital role in Nalini's own development, should have written his tribute to her and her art before he passed away. This series, then, is dedicated to the memory of Dr. Paul T. Lauby, missionary scholar and administrator for the advancement of Christian higher education in Asia, who died May 20, 2003, in Mount Holly, New Jersey, at the age of 78. He served from 1953 to 1969 as a United Church of Christ missionary at Silliman University in the Philippines. From 1969 until retirement in 1989 he was head of the United Board for Christian Higher Education in Asia.

Jonathan Bonk
Executive Director
Overseas Ministries Study Center
New Haven, Connecticut

Tribute

I take great delight in joining Nalini Jayasuriya's many friends around the world in celebrating the publication of this beautiful collection of her paintings and her accompanying commentary. This should provide the opportunity for many more people to be blessed by her unique art which conveys so much spiritual reality.

I became acquainted with Nalini some twenty years ago when she came from her native land, Sri Lanka, to study at Yale. It soon became apparent to me that she was a person of unusual spiritual depth and that she was able to express her insights vividly in her paintings and in her writing and music. Very soon she became a cherished friend. In 1985 the United Board with which I was connected was privileged to appoint her to the distinguished Elizabeth Luce Moore Professorship. As the Moore professor she communicated her faith as an artist in residence in Christian universities in Japan, the Philippines, and Thailand as well as at Yale Divinity School. Everywhere the response was enthusiastic. Then in 1988 Nalini was the prime mover in organizing a landmark conference of noted Asian artists and creative writers representing the great world religions. Nalini's moving keynote address created the open atmosphere for an exciting week of sharing.

I am pleased to have this opportunity to express once again my profound gratitude for all that Nalini has contributed to my life and to wish for her many more active years as an artist par excellence.

Paul T. Lauby
President Emeritus
United Board for Christian Higher
Education in Asia

The Art of Nalini Jayasuriya

Years ago a gentle knock on the door of my office at Yale Divinity School opened to a view of a south Asian woman in a blue sari. She introduced herself as Nalini Jayasuriya as I welcomed her. She explained that she was an artist from Sri Lanka and had come to Yale to study. That was early in the1980s. Little did I know that that little lady would bring a fresh vision of Christianity, a lively attitude about everything, a colorful artistic ability to her studies, and a worldview that would challenge everyone who was to meet her. After more than twenty years of acquaintance with her and her abilities, it is clear that many were changed by the visit of the little lady in the blue sari. In fact, those of us who know her and have followed her career have been changed by her, more than she has been changed by us.

It is her art that has kept getting in the way of how we have thought about the world, how we have thought about Asia, how we have thought about our own professions, and how we have thought about our religion.

Nalini Jayasuriya is a Christian believer, but her life situation, the mixed cultures she has been a part of, and especially the religious atmospheres that have matured her have made her a unique and multitalented citizen of the world. She has lived in many countries and cultures and has seen the world from many more points of view than the average citizen. It is remarkable that underneath the multicultural life she has lived is a deep, mystical, steadfast sense of being that resides in all that she does.

The first part of this book is about her art. She is a self-taught, self-made artist, but she has taken seriously many influences that have shaped her work. Her materials are rather simple. She prefers to work on cotton with bright colors in acrylic or watercolor paint. She seldom does very large works. She prefers that friends and acquaintances own her work or purchase it at very reasonable rates. She does not develop a wealthy clientele and earn great sums of money from her art.

Her drawings are an important part of her work, but they seldom get the recognition that her paintings receive. Nevertheless, two aspects of her drawings are important to consider when defining her abilities. In her drawings she works with a strong and clear line. The strength of her line drawings also shows the deep influence that South Asian images have had on her. Her drawings illustrate the original world from which she comes and, among other things, they show the powerful influence that Buddhist forms have had on her. Her drawings, always firm of line, are full of forms from her original culture.

Her paintings show the influence of the international life she has lived, but always they are filtered through that Sri Lankan lens that she values and to which she is loyal. It is true that much about contemporary Sri Lankan life gives Ms. Jayasuriya great unhappiness and disappointment, yet she holds an ideal in her mind of days past, of earlier friends, and of a Sri Lanka that in her heart is still her familiar Ceylon of old. This does not mean that Nalini lives only in the past, but it does mean that her memory of a more peaceful, mystical world is alive and well.

There are distinct and very different styles in her work, but each style, and there are three, is consistently maintained. I would call these three the animated, the impressionistic, and the existential.

The animated style is always more narrative and easier to read at first sight than the others. In this kind of work, Nalini deals with recognizable forms. It is also in this style that she has developed a Christian narrative. Her works that relate to the biblical story and to Christian hagiography are imaginative, challenging, and sometimes delightful. For instance, when she treats the biblical subject of the magi, she has made an imaginative presentation of the three figures that opens the story up to many interpretations and meanings. I refer to a specific painting that has the three magi, dressed in colorful Asian dress, on foot, rushing forward with gifts. While two of the figures carry something that is indistinct to the viewer, the first magi carries a white dove. The result in the painting is not that it perfectly interprets the scripture, but that it captures a spirit and an attitude about anticipation and wonder that leaves the observer rethinking the episode.

One of the most interesting paintings by Nalini in what I have called the animated style is a subject that she has painted more than once, one that is always referred to as "the Gospel." It is here that she challenges the viewer to think about what is in the painting and what it means.

Generally, she presents an attentive group dressed in imaginative Asian dress around a brightly lighted blond woman holding up a bird. The otherworldliness of such an image challenges the viewer to understand how this is a painting of the Gospel and, if it is true, what it means. It is in such a painting that Nalini brings the observer of her work into that mystical world that she insists is a part of all that she does.

While the narrative appears simple, the concept is radically new and challenges one to a way of thinking that is new. While a casual look at this animated style of painting may, to some, seem simplistic or odd, a careful consideration of what is coming through these works leaves one delighted and caught up in a worldview that is both refreshing and profound.

The second style that seems consistent in Ms. Jayasuriya's paintings is an impressionistic style that relies on color and suggestion more than on the precise lines of her drawings or the narrative power of her animated work. She works creatively with color. Still using the basic material of cotton and acrylic paints, she presents particular subject matter or scenes in highly suggestive ways.

For instance, the subject matter that lends itself to this style is the still life. Here she is less interested in a biblical or religious material, and presents the work as a pure visual statement. Her method is more suggestive than literal and her colors are more subdued and subtle than in the animated style. Her studies of bouquets of flowers are a case in point. There is less attention to a clear rendering of biological details than to the impression that a bouquet might mean to an observer. These images are more romantic and illusive of realism than any other aspect of her work.

For instance, a pearly white sphere surrounded by swirls of crimson, blue, and green suggests a delightful bouquet. Or a pearly white pitcher form beneath a burst of color suggests a still life bouquet. The emphasis here is on beauty as such rather than on a precise presentation of reality. Here the aesthetic comes into focus. These paintings are about a realm of knowing that is not captured by the artist by a presentation of reality as we know it; the art is about capturing images that relate to a reality that is different from what we know or can nail down with precision and details.

One enters a realm in Nalini Jayasuriya's work that is different from a commonplace reality, yet is recognizable through a lens that the artist puts on reality as we know it, in order to know or recognize something else, something new.

There is a more recent style in her work that seems to come from her exposure and attention to a world more distressful and unhappy than we have seen from her previously. I have referred to this style as the "existential." The works in this style have come later in her life and indicate that she has looked again at the suffering in her own world and has chosen to comment on it in her paintings that look again at the biblical story and find in it the places humanity has been cruel and inhuman to humanity.

I refer to her recent studies of St. Peter and his denial, and to her treatment of the suffering figure of Christ. She has chosen to treat the inhuman treatment of others through the well-known figures of the Christian tradition. Here, her style uses dark colors and forms in dramatic ways to express suffering.

For instance, there are images of St. Peter caught at the moment when he recognizes his own failure and weakness. In one image that I have in mind, St. Peter looks up at the observer with all his pain and self-knowing in his facial expression. This painting is devoid of beauty and attractiveness, but rather shows a human condition that is intolerable. In another of her studies of St. Peter, there is no facial expression to read; there is rather a bowed head, turned away from recognition and narrative impact. This study seems to me to be among the most courageous of her works, because it depends entirely on the observer's ability to enter into a human experience that is too painful even to illustrate. In this style she treats the figure of the suffering Christ in ways that are reminiscent of the medieval Christian tradition of the Suffering Servant. Her image of Christ is of one who is a victim, one who is maltreated. The Christ of her "existential" style is a quiet recipient of inhuman treatment. His suffering is to be contemplated, not because we see agony or mistreatment, but because we see a victim who stares at us and waits for a response. These paintings are not easy, yet they are profound attempts of the artist to comment on the contemporary world through what she appears to consider the icons of human suffering.

In the end, the three styles that mark the artistic work of Nalini Jayasuriya appear to be the worlds that she has integrated into her own vision, namely, the world of animated figures that narrate some of the ancient stories of the Christian tradition through a multicultural lens, the expressionistic world of beauty that calls for the observer to look beyond reality to other realities, and finally to see also an existential world where the human condition cries out at its treatment of itself.

John W. Cook
Guilford, Connecticut

Paintings

they hear the music
they follow
I hear; I do not follow
but the Prophet plays on and on
knowing that some day
I will hear and follow
as my stilled unsearching mind unfolds

Then
I will hear
and the Prophet's song
will be mine.

Prophet

gold of sunrise garnet streaked
pinned into amethyst jasper turquoise
bright carnelian sapphire pearl
vision written with sunset rubies . . .

wrapped in an emerald rainbow
bound in adoring song
my Icon of Faith
my wordless Prayer
my Offering through illumined time . . .

Mary
Mother of Christ
Hear me . . .

Icon

Matthew sees
Luke ponders
Mark witnesses
John dreams

Matthew will speak in forms
Luke will outline wonder
Mark will burn words into everlasting Time
and John will dream
through the dazzling unfolding wine dark night

as the Dream of generations
sweeps through the soundless darkness
to reveal the fire
of a new Revelation . . .

The Gospels

Strong turquoise stones
from her snow mountain
her rosary retelling her words of wonder
counting adoring words of mountain prayer
as the evening leaves
with ruby lighted feet . . .

in whispering light
her illumined offering for another day
as darkness trails a purple light of silence
over her blessed snow mountain . . .

Evensong

Unknowing; from Nowhere
now asleep:
the Magi in Search of the Miraculous.

awakened by the Angel they see the Star
the Star that will lead them to Bethlehem . . .

now they ride the flying clouds
soaring ecstatic
to know the wonder
of the Word reborn
to touch again
the wonder of Revelation.

Magi Sleeping

unnumbered numbered
flowing weaving sounds
words answering words threaded ordered
sprinkled measured stars in a patterned sky
in chasing lines into arcs into spinning circles

reminding sound
voices recalling answering memory
voices alight retelling memory
weaving unweaving magical webs
seducing silence
into silent wonder . . .

Fugue

poor Judas
executioner; brutal hangman of Judas . . .

does he know
can he know
that a Drop of Redeeming Blood
from a Pierced Hand
is falling into his unutterable darkness . . .

he hunted himself
fettered in his conflict
did he hunt himself or his unrelenting shadow . . .

belonging
only to himself
lost in his own darkness

and we
unseeing
in our own Darkness
do we
cast the first stone . . .

Is My Name Judas?

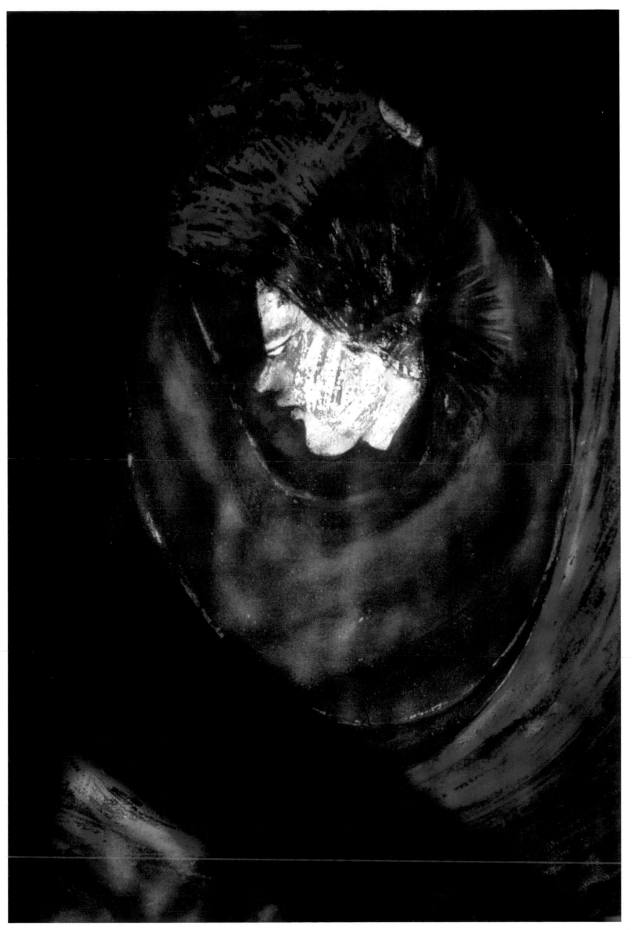

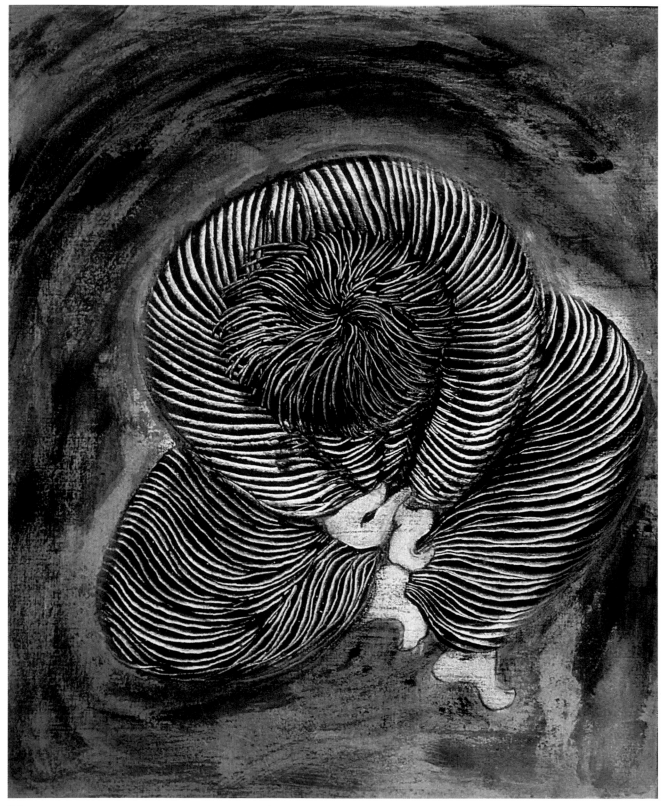

not my way but the way you have pointed
not my scepter but the scepter given
not my robe but the ordered robe of tears
not my crown
but a fire of thorns . . .

not my tree but the first Tree of Eden:
ordained, ordered I bow; obey unquestioning:

not my will but Yours
my Father
my God . . .

Gethsemane

Hosanna in the Highest
Behold the King
Blessed is He who comes in the Name of the Lord . . .

what shall I do then with this man
you call your King?
Crucify Him they shouted.
Why? He asked: but they shouted louder
Crucify Him, Crucify Him—
let His blood
be upon us and our children . . .

Hosanna

does Satya speak
does Satya play
does Satya sing unspoken words

free
unbound I wait
lost in the wonder of seamless silence
lost in the sacred seamless silence
of Satya's song . . .

my soul
magnifies the Lord
and my spirit rejoices
in God my Saviour

Satya = Sanskrit for Truth

Circled in sacred words:
dreaming together
knowing together
the numinous wonder
enclosing Mary . . .

Annunciation

where you go I will go
your people will be my people
your land my land
your god my god . . .

my faithfulness
neither demands nor binds
my faithfulness
is a Freedom
beyond all knowing

Ruth and Naomi

Even if I have to die with you, he insisted
I will never disown you . . .
surely not me, Rabbi . . .

Is it me Lord?
Surely not me

No, no—never: how could I deny you . . .
Who do you say that I am?
You are the Christ
Son of the Living God . . .

No
I do not know this man . . .

Is it me?
But I am Peter—
Is my name Judas . . . ?

The Meal

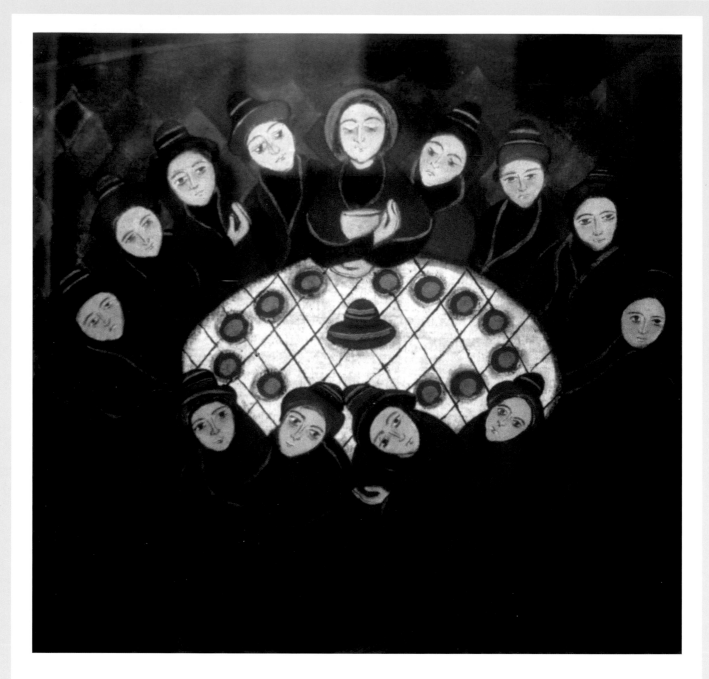

Is the Banquet ending
and will the Chosen One leave
leaving his royal purple hat?

The Bread and the Drink
will remain on the table

they know
He will return

Banquet

Is the little king sleeping
knowing the holy silence of the angels—
knowing the holy awe
the holy love
of Mary his blessed Mother . . .

Is the Little King Sleeping

my darkness
rests upon your Word
so let me come into the midst of your conversation
with pointed dancing feet writing my prayer
my arms imploring to be enclosed
within your Presence . . .

in burning light
this spinning axis spins my faith
into your Presence
witness to the Witness you are in my life . . .

Dance

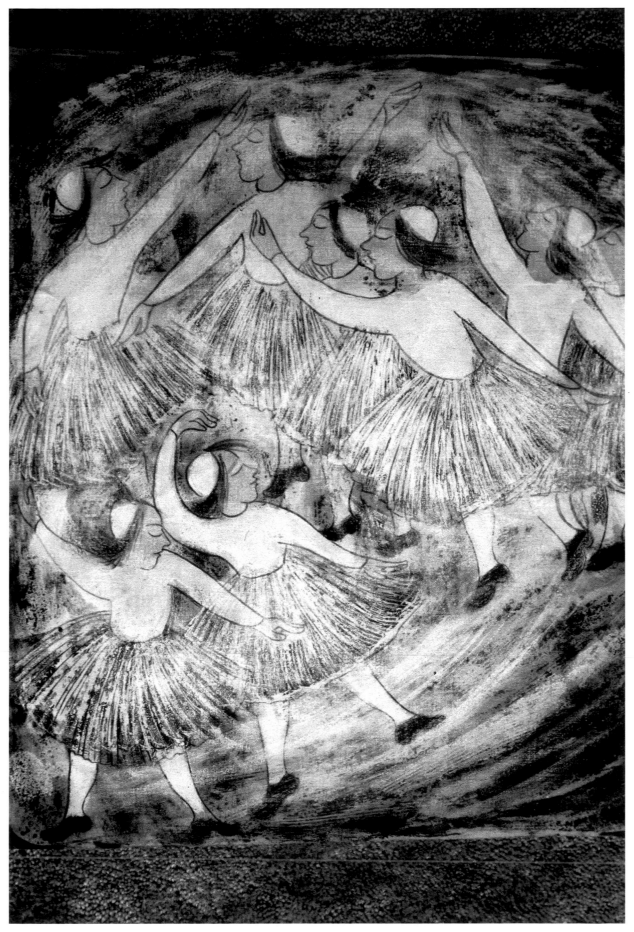

who is this braided with stars
this sudden unspeaking radiant youth
with garnet eyes
this mercurial dazzling
Form of Light . . .

I know this Face with bloodied stripes
I know
this shredded silent Face
reviled
rejected
abandoned
alone

thrown to the night

Jesus Christ

Centered
in His own Centre
absorbed absorbing
not in Time or Space . . .

Being and Becoming
His Form
Majestic in Holiness
Awesome in Glory
The Name
Illuming the Sun

Mandala, the squared Circle is Sanskrit
for Centre and Circle—the ceaseless expanding
Centre into beginless endless circles, absorbing
the predictable and ordered structures
of existence, with no reference to Time or Space;
silencing the mind and freeing the spirit
in a search for the Miraculous—

This is my adaptation of an ancient visual
diagram used by prophets and priests in
ancient Tibet, to silence the speculating mind,
to know again the lost and the unknown

Ancient wisdom sometimes unwraps its
magical secrecy, and its mythical and
mysterious disciplines may unfold the
hiddenness of wonder and the wonder of
Wonder itself . . .

Christ Mandala

in this silence, uninformed
summoning every moment
known and unknowing
flying through the door of the Sun

now
I am become
what I know
I am

released from
my nest of
stones
dazzling
I am again
a butterfly

Silence

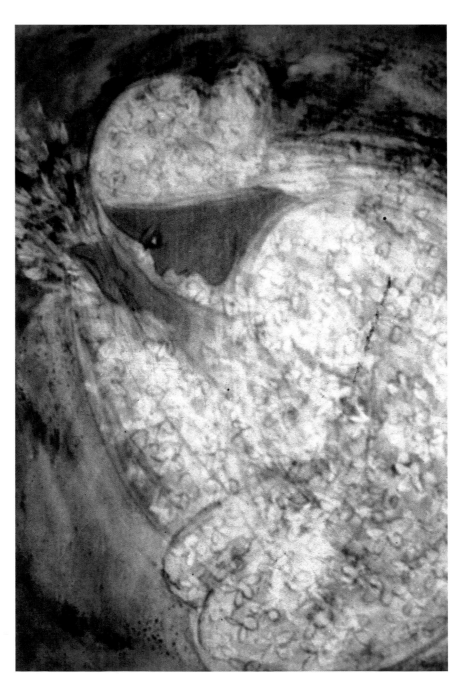

in the awakened Garden
Adam and Eve
woven together into Oneness:
rejoicing weeping
through all the seasons of returning Time
in raining flowers
in dancing light
held in the sacred promise the holy radiance
adorning life

The Garden

The small bird wished to speak to the
holy mountain—but she was only a
small bird.

One day she took her long silk scarf in
her beak and flew upwards, upwards in
the sky to the summit of the mountain,
touching it as she flew—
and she knew
the mighty Rock had heard her silk . . .

The birds of the world were troubled
that they had not found God anywhere.
So they flew to heaven in a great singing cloud;
and they searched and searched;
and they were deeply disappointed
they had not found God anywhere in Heaven . . .
So they flew back to the world—and
there was God waiting for them,
waiting for them in the world!

The Birds

the Word
rose from the mighty waters
rose a tree
wrapped in a circling rainbow—
the rainbow danced
lifting the sky
spilling its jewels across the earth
spilling the jeweled drops into birds:
flashing wondrous walking swimming birds
soaring birds, singing
singing
in a singing Tree

Tree

Both these tales are adapted from Eastern wisdom.

And Jesus came and said to them, "All authority in heaven and on earth has been given to me. Go therefore and make disciples of all nations, baptizing them in the name of the Father and of the Son and of the Holy Spirit, and teaching them to obey everything that I have commanded you. And remember, I am with you always, to the end of the age."
Matthew 28:18—20

The Great Commission

"Rejoice with me, for I have found my sheep that was lost."
Luke 15:6

Christ

"Then Joseph got up, took the child and his mother by night, and went to Egypt . . ."
Matthew 2:14

Flight into Egypt

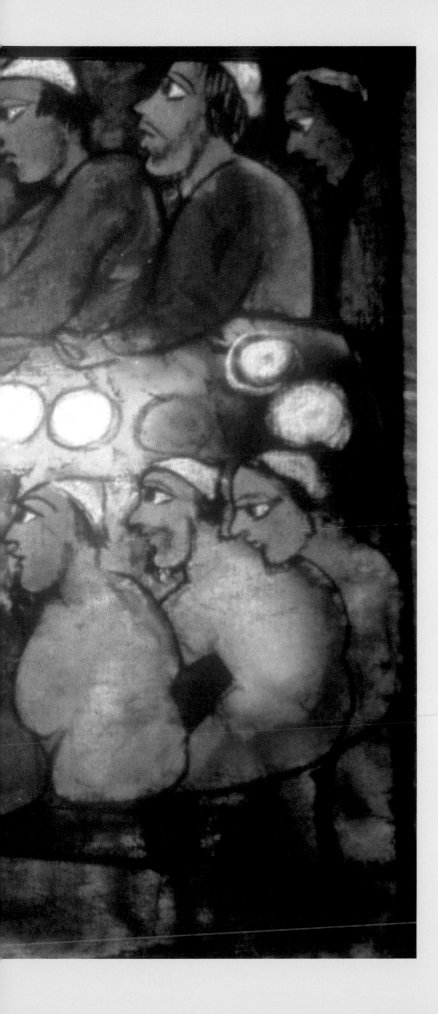

"While they were eating, he took a loaf of bread, and after blessing it he broke it, gave it to them, and said, 'Take; this is my body.' Then he took a cup, and after giving thanks he gave it to them, and all of them drank from it."
Mark 14:22–23

The Last Supper

"Then, opening their treasure chests, they offered him gifts of gold, frankincense, and myrrh."
Matthew 2:11

Magi

The gifts he gave were that some would be . . . evangelists . . .
Ephesians 4:11

Evangelists

"The angel said to her, 'Do not be afraid, Mary, for you have found favor with God. And now, you will conceive in your womb and bear a son, and you will name him Jesus."
Luke 1:30–31

Mother and Child

"When he was at the table with them, he took bread, blessed and broke it, and gave it to them. Then their eyes were opened, and they recognized him; and he vanished from their sight."
Luke 24:30–31

The Emmaus Road

Reminiscences

Witness of a Life

When you have watched the sunrise you thank God
When you have seen the great circular baptismal
Window of light of John Piper, in Coventry Cathedral in
England, you thank God for the wonder He inspires.

The Circle, beginless and endless is the prime symbol of the East
The Visual Arts revolve in it
Words reappear in it
Sound returns in it
Dance, in ceaseless cyclic rhythms
Dances again

Life is a Circle with its circumference everywhere
And its Centre Nowhere

I search for Understanding:
I search this Nowhere
I search for the Centre . . .

I know the Centre exists

Wind has voices
Rain has voices
Silence has many voices
And the Sea speaks
With all these voices . . .

As Time spread lighted wings and flew over all the world, the Voice spoke
And I heard, as I stood listening on the Seashore of the world
"Go," the voice ordered. "Do not walk in the footprints you see.
Make your own footprints in the Sand.
This will be your Covenant and your Reward"

The Sea flows in my veins.
The Sea breathes in me.
In this timeless spaceless power I live and live again, knowing that all Life
    Death and Return are a Wave of the Sea . . .

I watch the sea for hours, listening learning from its rhythms and moods.

The wave rises, singing its power—lighted, rising upward, soaring to its
    climax.

Suddenly it falls, crashing into itself, and spreading in a circle of silent
    foam—
But it returns to the Sea; it is another wave, becoming again and again,
    dancing the shore in brightness . . .

Murti, the Asian concept of ceaseless Becoming, is the Sea.
The Sea is: and is forever becoming . . .

It is not surprising that many people find the East difficult to understand.
Unlike the West where definition is precise and meaning is unclouded,
    Eastern expression is complex, visionary and spacious.
The East resists inquiry and may appear uncompromising; and may not be
    fully understood through reasoning, opposition or debate

The religions and philosophies of the East are many-layered and involved,
    and result from a meditative understanding of life.
As in the visual art and sculpture of the East, form and expression are
    suggested, not disclosed.

There is a Secrecy within all Eastern expression—an ancient sacramental
    and elusive secrecy . . .

Offering

Today we are part of the unremitting continuance of illumined consciousness
    known as Religion. In every culture this wisdom has been revealed in
    distinctive ways, retold through sound and silence, enacted in ritual and
    liturgy, and recalled endlessly through every creative form.

To witness to these with gratitude is the inspiring and informing purpose of
    all sacred expression in visual form, movement, sound and silence: but
    within the expression of every religion and wisdom teaching of the human
    race, however much they differ, is a unified intention to reveal that there
    is in the world a much greater power than ourselves.

Carl Jung has said that modern man does not understand how much his
    rationalism has destroyed his capacity to respond to the Numinous, and
    to the development of his intuitive capacity so necessary to spiritual
    growth.
The holy power of religious story, symbol, ritual, ordinance and belief
    celebrate together the Multiplicity Oneness and Noneness of the creative
    sacred enterprise of the world
All sacred expression invites participation, links people, fulfills human needs
    and unites believers in enduring bonds of hope and confidence.

The spiritual intelligence of all wisdom teachings has always interested me
    deeply.
In Hindu belief the cosmos and the human body are functional variants of
    the same energy pattern—
This ancient belief was re-echoed by the great contemporary scientist, Carl
    Sagan, when he said we are all made of the stuff of stars

There is a deeply profound Asian concept that defines in Sanskrit what we
    know as spiritual.

It explains that *Sukshma Sharira*, or subtle aspect, describes the inner world of ideas thoughts and perceptions, visions and dreams.

It is in this inner world of the heart where the Hindu god Shiva dances, in a periodical recovery of beginnings.

Hovering between the elemental and the sublime, man searches the pathless way to freedom—
Will he ever find it?
Will he ever silence his mind well enough to know himself?

There is wonder in all the sacred expression of the whole world—it is all momentous and worthy of respect: because it is witness to the precious emotion known as Belief that is as real as life itself.

There is a singing dancing pictorial anxiety in man that compels him to record his moments of revelation—and all the artists of the world have reinterpreted these truthfully into becoming our inheritance of holy wonder.

To hear a Cantata in the sacred space of Sancta Maria Maggiore, to behold the opulence of San Vitale and the power of Gothic architectural ascent and the glass-lighted stone of Chartres, to have remembered in Gethsemane, to stand in the silence of the Gal Vihare in the once royal capital in Sri Lanka—the silence of the long supreme sleeping stone Buddha form; to sit on the ancient stone floor of a mountain temple, becoming one of the many-toned chant of one hundred seated Buddhist monks; to breathe the scent of wild jasmine above the pink and purple lotus opening on the water, and to watch a turquoise azure cloud of peacocks dancing in the sun: I could go on speaking of these endlessly—
This has been my privilege for which I thank God

Because I know that it was each miracle He set alight that illumined my own life—
And these Memoirs are an opportunity to give thanks, and to remember with gratitude, all the individuals and institutions in several countries who have helped the miracles to order my life in such extraordinary ways.

I am an Asian, and I think and contemplate life as an Asian. And I write as an Asian—
I hope you will try to understand.

Now, here at the Overseas Ministries Study Center, I have been offered the privilege of writing my Memoirs.

I am yet not certain why, because I always thought memoir writing was for important people.

Is it because my life, outside the runways of the predictable and ordered, has surfaced and found resolution in most unexpected ways?
It has.
And no one has been as surprised as I have been.

As a little child I watched every dawn on the sea with my father, and every dawn was a radiant beginning.

Then on one dark September day he was suddenly not there. I was alone and afraid. And I was lost.
Because my only friend was not there beside me in the dawn.

My retreat was in our great Tulip Tree; and as I sat in its comforting silence I wondered if the Voice would speak again.

Was there something else I needed to know
Was there some hope of a future in this closing darkness:
Could something happen to lift this failing spirit?

The metaphor for most helpless people is to shine even precariously for a moment—and there is a yearning angst for a future however vague . . .

Would there ever come a time for my singing?

I sat in my tree for long hours wondering—neither seeing nor knowing; nor understanding . . .
So how could I ever have guessed that the future I had not dared to hope for was already a point of light in the darkness—
And somewhere within that bright reality would be the opportunity to exceed myself—
The bidding word was Miracle . . .

Memoirs are of Life and Life is Stories
Without stories life would be an inexorable process of existence punctuated by birth death, and the events between

In Asia, the best is not always the winner: wealth power and family usually make, or are used to making the decisions.

Now, at my age, I realize what lasting joy there is in helping others, especially the poor, we find in our part of the world.
And it is also true that the pain we give to others is a nail we drive into our own hearts—
Guilt seldom heals: when it does, scars remain

I believe we are who we were in a lived time of our ancestors.
In writing these memoirs I shall speak of my family and my ancestors, and there may be echoes of them in me.

To write these stories of a faded past is the unlocking of an old house with
  relics of the past, meaningless and insignificant today . . . But it is
  important to visit them in these past centuries, to learn of the prejudices
  and pride that harmed so many; and to understand who we are and why
  we are today.

Stories weaving and unweaving our lives through darkness and light, tell us
  also who we might have been and who we have become.

Time orders Life, binding it sometimes with a band of steel, sometimes with a
  skein of water: and the unfailing truth of Mortality is the ace Time deals,
  so that its presence and power are never ignored.

I am grateful for the opportunity to speak also about Sri Lanka, this most
  beautiful country I come from, with its romantic and legendary
  beginnings and its ancient documented history and culture of over two
  thousand five hundred to three thousand years.

This Garden of Eden, as it has often been described, is a place of surprises
  and contrasts; but the gentle undemanding wisdom teachings of
  Buddhism have left their sublime and persuasive influence.

> Friends
> like stars in the sky
> stars in the water
> always there—
> pinned to the darkness
> dancing the night . . .
>
> Friends
> like stars threading the darkness
> always;
> always in the sky
> and in the water . . .

These Memoirs are a Tribute to my Friends from many countries of the world,
  and also from my own Sri Lanka.
These are people, now a memorable part of my life, who have been and are,
  my Blessing and my Gift.

The Memoirs are also an Offering to my parents and my brother, who taught
  me how to live with grace and dignity, and with honour.

*   *   *   *

I have for very long been interested in the Sacred Arts of the world confessing
  faith, and leaving a reminding presence of that faith.

one grain of rice down and pushed it all the way to her home; then
another and another and another . . .
Out of the corner of her eye, Amme saw I was asleep, kissed my small feet as
she always did, unrolled her mat, chanted her Buddhist stanzas and
went to sleep; dear honest gentle storyteller who taught me so much . . .

The Magician and the Clown are important, especially in Asia, as they appear
in the systems that govern and order existence.
They are very real.
The Magician makes everything happen that does not happen.

The Clown, with his mask, thinks he makes everything happen that does not
happen . . .
One day, he sets his mask aside, looks in the mirror and sees his own face
for the first time; and he wonders who it is who looks back at him.
Accustomed to one and now intrigued by the other he sits wondering . . .
Will he know himself without his mask—and if he wears it again, will he
continue hiding himself from himself?

                    *   *   *   *

I Believe.
That was the title of the lecture I was invited recently to give at Cambridge
University in England. I felt privileged to be speaking to a scholarly and
distinguished audience in a country that had offered me my first
opportunity for further education.

I have lectured often before Western audiences, and I have sometimes
wondered what it is for them to hear me, an Asian Christian, from a
predominantly Buddhist culture, who has also absorbed some of the
wonder of non-Christian concepts and visions.
I am glad to say the response has always been encouraging.

I Believe. With an exultant certainty, in every language spoken and
unspoken, the human race has made this exalted confession of faith.

I believe; help thou my unbelief; Thou the Beginless Beginning.
What compelling power sets aside the rational logical reality that orders life
and believes in a Word, a Vision or a Memory—what is it that takes man
beyond himself in Search of the Miraculous?

In Asia, Creation is continuous as God is—a Power symbolized by the
beginless endless Circle, contained and containing, renewed and
renewing in itself.
Nothing is considered conclusive or attained in Asian thought except the
freedom from conclusion and attainment.
In the manifold diversity of Asian peoples, and the extent and immediacy of
their creative response to revelation, is a splendour of differences; but at
the secret core of all witness is the unseen, the unknown, the   unnamed
and many-named Numinous Being.

The Christian declares, "I believe in God and His Son Jesus Christ."

The Muslim proclaims, "There is no god but God and Mohammed is his Prophet."

The Hindu encompasses all creation as he prays, "God is our life."

Buddhism alone, without reference to any Being, teaches the value of the enlightened mind, saying, "Look within, there is the Buddha."

Determination and Resolution are fine Western attributes; the fluent Asian mind is elusive: Wonder is experienced and expressed through forms and metaphors that are within or beyond mediation.

And, the ordered mind would say, one plus one equals two—esoteric Asian expression would suggest, one plus one, is the beginning of Infinity . . .

In the 1960's the "Is God dead?" debate was on, and the new generations believed there was nothing mysterious or hidden that science could not explain.
Art and Religion were valued as meeting psychological needs and as patterns for correct behaviour, and everything was predictable and could be known.

But, some fifty thousand years ago, the prehistoric artist hunter drawing the form of his food animal on the darkest wall of his cave, believed he had, in capturing its form, cast a spell over it that would enable him to hunt it down. He sensed through some fear or some enigmatic memory, a mysterious unknowing within and around him . . .
Fifty thousand years later, the great scientist, Albert Einstein declared that the most profound emotion we can experience is the perception of the mystical; it is to know that what seems impenetrable, really exists.

Asians have a great capacity for intellectual and spiritual pursuits, and many thousands of manuscripts, some on palm leaves, remain as the research and reflection of scholarly monks and laymen.
The search for a deeper understanding of life and its purpose never ends— most Asians think and reflect deeply, most deeply perhaps in their hearts.
The mysterious and elusive pervade Eastern Life, and the rich and diverse concepts and expressions are absorbed through the meditative disciplines of Contemplation: the ultimate hope is to arrive at an understanding of absolute Truth beyond all concepts and expressions.
Multiplicity, Oneness and Noneness are celebrated through the holy power of ancient ritual and myth, and the forms through which the East and West find understanding differ.

So the imperialist, Rudyard Kipling saying, "East is East and West is West," might have been sensible, as one finds that in the East, *Space is Existence, Time is Experience, Thought is Cosmic Adventure, and Maya, the most controversial, is Illusion, that Is and Is Not.*
Sacred form is celebrated endlessly, recalling and honouring the Holy Being.
Buddhism outlines the concept of non form, and Buddhism celebrates Absence.
The Asian strives to escape his selfhood—to subvert the ego and free himself from consequential Samsara or the cycle of Rebirth and Reappearance.
In sharp contrast, the Magi appear, seeking the miracle of a new creation. *"Behold, I make all things new."*

The sacred expression of the West is confident and triumphalistic: sacred Eastern confession is introspective; it is an art of Invocation inspired by a spiritual knowledge transcending reason.

The Hindu affirms belief
The Buddhist sifts reality
The Christian confesses faith
The Muslim proclaims submission
Proverbs says, "The Lord possessed me in the beginning of my way"—the way to the reality and Presence of God . . .
In all religions, the Divine reality is confessed instinctively. And in Dr. David Ford's book, *Self and Salvation*, he looks with three other scholars at the Face of Jesus—the *Ecce Homo* of Georges Rouault
For twenty centuries the world has seen Jesus glorified, transfigured sorrowful dying—sublime; unanswering, even in death . . .
Since I was a child I saw this face; to me it was another holy picture.

In 1979, in the class of Professor John Wesley Cook at Yale, my whole being was summoned to look at the Face—the dead face of Jesus in the Isenheim altarpiece of fifteenth-century Mathis Grunewald.

In an unbelievable silence the class heard the professor's words—a few—as we were confronted by a dead leprous alienated face—an abused face; the Face of Jesus Christ.
Here was no theology of the Cross.
It was for me the terrifying truth of sin and unrelenting evil.
The face sobbed; the tears of the tormented face were for those who would, through the centuries, stand before it.

Professor Cook taught without words, the suffering and abandonment of Jesus Christ . . .
Determinism is a brutal law prohibiting thought and stifling freedom.
Jesus defied the rigorous determinism of state and religion and suffered the consequences: and his suffering has bound the Christian world into a suffering of remorse through centuries.
It has been said that the Face and the theology it inspires is the power of religion.

Georges Rouault asks us to Behold the Man—
Does the Man ask, "Who are you?" of the beholding world?
No. He asks, "Who am I?"
And he awaits our answer . . .

* * * *

Amongst primal people there is a might of wisdom and an enduring bond of rituals, beliefs and customs in an interrelated Totality.

An ancient belief is that what appears opposed can belong together in the immensity of Oneness.

This ideal equilibrium affords balance and harmony—the balance and harmony of the renewing earth and sky, and the returning sun moon and stars.

Life needs a Tomorrow of expectation—an impulse that speeds humanity beyond the repeated and the known.

As Professor John Cook has said, "Art is perceived through ecstasy where one's sensibilities are stretched to the realization of a mystical reality."

There is a pictorial anxiety in man; a persistent memory, and a need to record significant ideas and experience; a need to seize into witness the moment between illusion and reality and pin its transforming wonder on the human race.

Science presents Facts—Sacred vision manifested in Art is Disclosure, as man tries to understand the truth about himself and his place in the world's order.
According to Archaeology, there was many thousands of years ago a centrifugal movement of various tribes of people into various distances and vast stretches of land and water. With this movement, the human race is known to have dispersed into resulting and separate ways; however, universal myths of Space, Time and Experience, and shared beliefs of Life, Death and Renewal remained, sustaining life and maintaining moral and religious orders and beliefs.

The needs of all people are the same.
They need protection from fear and a hope for blessing; and these are rested universally in a Saviour God.
There is a galaxy within us—an unpredictable portion of our being, beyond the constraints of the rational and the reasonable that can surprise the world with profound expressions of faith.
This is revelation of Truth, illumined and transforming as it informs and sanctifies. And all the world's wisdom teaching and creative expression have endured, because Truth is the living center of these.

Most of Asia is a multitude of forms sounds colours movements and beliefs, and not surprisingly, its most honoured Wisdom Teaching, Buddhism, presents itself most eloquently through its Silence.

Hinduism, Buddhism, Christianity and Islam are amongst the major religions practised in Sri Lanka, and I have watched some of their practices and rituals and have been awed by the intensity of their beliefs.

I have watched Hindu devotees in a frenzy of belief walk barefoot on great burning coals of fire, and pierce deep patterns on their flesh: they do not burn and they do not bleed.

Buddhist hermit monks deep in the jungles sit meditating for several days without food or water.

The new convert begs crucifixion to glorify God; and the Muslim blows himself up honouring the name of Allah—

Are these only evidence and entitlements of reckless loyalty, or witness of an awesome power of Faith?

*   *   *   *

The Little Bird and the Silken Scarf

The little bird looked far far up at the Great Mountain in the sky, and she sang "I will fly over the Mountain."

The forest shook with derisive laughter.

The little bird whispered to the Great Mountain and asked for a long silken scarf; and very soon, a long silken scarf floated down.

The little bird picked one corner of the scarf in her tiny beak and flew upwards into the sky.

She flew higher and higher, rising with the silk scarf to the summit of the Great Mountain.

Then, with all her strength, she rose and flew over the summit with her silken scarf behind her.

The mocking forest bowed its head.

And the little bird flapped her small wings with deep thankfulness and joy—

And she knew the Great Mountain had heard her silk.

*   *   *   *

Sound as Word is the vital element in religion. "In the beginning was the Word."

In Hinduism, the sacred syllable *Om* affirms God is our Life; and Buddhist chant by monks in Sri Lanka in a wide range of rhythmic sound is magical.

I have heard the muezzin call the faithful to prayer in many Islamic countries—a call that echoes and re-echoes five times a day . . .

And the bells of temple, church, minaret and mosque summon humanity to awaken and acknowledge God.

> *Hinduism encompasses*
> *Buddhism absorbs*
> *Christianity discloses*
> *Islam conceals and reveals*

In Sri Lanka these surround us with their holiness and sanctify us with their wisdom. Their presence illumines our land and blesses all our people.

I am a musician.

My interest has been in teaching, being taught, and learning to listen to the sounds I hear, and to listen to my own understanding of these.
Sound has deep significance for me.
The Sounds of Nature, of wind and water, of creatures awakening in our abundant jungles; the sound of the sea and the sound of its silence, resonant and reminding, are the voices of our island, unique and beautiful.

I have had the privilege of hearing some of the world's greatest orchestras and performers under their revered conductors in England, Germany, France, Italy, the United States, Russia, Japan, Israel, and other countries.

The Royal Festival Hall in London was one of my favourite places in the time I studied in London. To hear Madrigals sung by British singers was always a rare and exquisite experience.

J. S. Bach's *St. Matthew Passion* and Handel's *Messiah* sung in German were for me an early experience of the holy power of massed voices, never freeing the hearer from its might of passion and its tender solicitude. Among other glorious performances (or should I say offerings) were several opportunities to hear with almost incredible wonder the musicians from the East, Midori, Yo Yo Ma and others, and our own world famous pianist, Malini Peiris and cellist Rohan de Saram, now accompanied by his brilliant brother Druvi, whom I had the pleasure of teaching at S. Thomas' College in Sri Lanka.

There are many others, too many to name here; but they remain remembered: but I cannot, I may not let this moment pass without returning to a couple of other sounds—one of collective structured perfection in Rome, and the other in the winter snow of the Himalayas.

I had been in the Vatican before to stand in awe of the immortal offerings of da Vinci, Michelangelo, Donatello and so many others. But that day, when I heard the chant of plainsong by a myriad voices in the Sistine Chapel, I can only describe it as a cosmic experience.

I did not see the chanting people or know who they were. It did not matter then nor does it now—so many years later; but the wonder will remain alive and resonant in me.

Samye is the oldest Tibetan Buddhist monastery, eighteen thousand feet in the Himalayas above Kathmandu, and in Kathmandu is Syambonath, the oldest Buddhist temple that stands within its prayer wheel walls and thousands of prayer flags fluttering above and around its graceful contours.

That day, no one was permitted to enter Syambonath, so I remained outside with the waiting crowd of Tibetan and Nepalese worshippers, tourists and visitors. Then from afar, a long line of brown-robed Tibetan monks wearing their very wide brimmed hats and walking slowly began to appear.

There were one hundred of them.

They had walked from Samye for several hours to light the hundred small oil lamps around the great bronze Buddha image inside the Syambonath: to chant and worship in this ancient sacred space of silence.

As we watched, the monks arrived, unlaced their footwear and threw these and their hats on the stone floor.

Seated in a circle, they remained with their shaven heads deeply bowed for a long while: then a soft gong was sounded. They rose, filled the lamps with the butter they had brought, and the hundred monks lighted the hundred little oil lamp wicks.

In a little while the great bronze Buddha image in silent meditation glowed; the monks returned to their circle, sat cross-legged and meditated.

Then, as if from the heart of the mountains, one voice chanted the recitative, and the single sound became many. They then came in, one by one, the hundred voices chanting in overtones; a sound sublime infinite timeless—gathering the silence of all life to witness the celebration of the enlightened knowledge of an Enlightened Being; the Buddha who revealed the truth of both Reality and Unreality.

In this sacred space, entranced and captured by the experience of such
    profound and moveless witness, I sank to the cold stone floor, deeply
    grateful to have heard such sound and silence; and I remained there for a
    long while.

The monks moved out as silently as they had entered, returning to Samye
    and their own contemplative silence in the Himalayan snows.

And I remained in that experience for a very long while . . . .

There are many Hindu festivals that are celebrated throughout India and in
    several countries of Asia where many Hindus live, as in Sri Lanka; and
    these must rank among the most colourful processions, as vibrant
    insistent flutes and drums accompanying fire twirlers, holy men and
    frenzied dancers, intense and overcome with a sacred ecstasy, perform on
    the main streets.

This is known as Vel, and is the movement of sacred images between two
    Hindu temples.

Holi, a delightful Spring festival happens in India, when hundreds of
    beautiful paper kites fill the sky amidst great rejoicing.

Throughout Asia, sacred and secular celebration is most colourful and
    intensely alive with ethnic dance and music. It is a joyous response and a
    celebration of life. To the millions in Asia who suffer from great poverty,
    the colour and drama of life are in its ceremonies.

Bathing in the sacred Ganges is an obligation for the Hindu believer. During
    a festival called Kumbh Mela, several millions of Hindus immerse
    themselves, and as in the sacred circling of Muslim pilgrims round the
    Ka'aba in Mecca, many have died in the stampede that often occurs at
    the beginning of the festival, when emotions are alight with a fierce
    religious intensity.

I have had the privilege of seeing nearly all the oldest and most beautiful
    mosques of the Islamic world.

Islam is believed to have prohibited visual representation of any life form, so
    the decorative schemes of dome, wall, ceiling and floor of sacred space,
    are abstracted forms, of a variety and richness that are incredible.

The most amazing is the art of calligraphy, where the words of the Koran,
    inlaid and ornamented, are a spiritual geometry unsurpassed in its skill
    and beauty.
Some of the most exquisitely decorated mosques I have seen were in Shiraz
    and Isfahan in Iran, and there are many spectacularly beautiful mosques
    in several countries of the world . . .

The Badshahi mosque is old and beautiful. From the road below, I watched ten thousand Muslims perform their sequence of worship in this great mosque in the beautiful old city of Lahore in Pakistan. This was in the courtyard outside; I do not know how many men were inside the mosque.

In the final act of supplication all the rows of these worshipping thousands bowed together as one man; it was like the mightiest wave of the sea: the order and the synchronization were awesome.

Asia has an amazingly diverse and rich cultural heritage.

To the West it may appear strangely exciting but remote. It is all this and more. And in its witness is a profound expression of an ancient and dazzling cultural heritage.

The esoteric expression of Islam, secret still to a great extent, has produced beautiful contemplative literature and the rare exquisite beauty of Rumi's poetry.

The prophet Mevlana, who set himself free from the institutionalized forms of Islamic worship was rare, creative and unafraid.

A poet and artist himself and a true believer in Islam, Mevlana the prophet, knew the wonder of form, movement and sound that were visionary and original, and meaningful.

In Konya in Turkey, where Mevlana was born, there are annual celebrations of his birth; and I had the great joy of attending one of these with Dr. Ibrahim, an old Turkish surgeon, and Ms. Sofi Huri, a Greek Christian publisher.
And it was there that I saw Mevlana's Whirling Dervishes.

We were escorted into a very very large hall at the far end of which was a dais with a large covered seat. On it, with legs crossed, sat an old bearded man like a king, in ivory-coloured robes; and on his head was a great turban of silk.

Sofi and I were the only women present, and there were several hundreds of men wearing caps and white flowing clothes seated on the floor in curving lines. The three chairs facing the dais were ours, and in front of us was a large empty space.

The large hall was very silent.

Then, very quietly a beautiful sound like a deep contralto grew and moved— it was the voice of the *Nayh*, a Turkish woodwind, being blown by a young musician; and then the old man on the dais began to sing in a deep rich voice.

The audience listened, spellbound by the voice of the singer and the voice of the Nayh.

From a door to our left they came in single file; small boys, youths and young men dressed in white cotton tunics and trousers and knee length accordion-pleated skirts. On their feet were small black shoes, and they wore slightly conical black caps, each with a long tassel.

The voice and the Nayh grew in hypnotic sound, and the forty Dervishes who had come in were walking in patterns slowly at first, then growing faster—moving faster and faster—whirling in whirling patterns—whirling so fast that the slightly tilted bodies in white were swirling clouds all over the room.
Sometimes they slowed down for a few moments, then, gathering speed their blurred forms in constant movement, they whirled again and again over the circle of space that had waited for them . . .

For twenty-six minutes the Whirling Dervishes whirled—their right arms with open palms raised to heaven, and their left arms with palms facing downwards to the earth—receiving the power of God into their bodies and returning it to the earth . . .

The whirling slowed down and quietly ended; and the Dervishes, in a quietly moving line moved out through the open door . . . It was over. Their hour of sacred witness had been completed.

The audience still very silent moved out.

The great space was empty and the Nayh whispered its soft farewell.

The old man on the dais bowed in silence; and the aura of exquisite sound seemed to enclose him.

We rose to leave. We were silent too.

We had seen and heard a prayer to God and we had all known a moment of holiness . . .

Oberammergau is a small village not too far from Munich where I had worked with the famous artist Professor Hans Gotfried von Stockhausen in the studios of Karl Mayer, a great name in stained glass.

The Mayer family, like many in Southern Germany, were very kind and generous to me, and knowing my thoughts, gave me the opportunity of seeing the world-famous Passion Play in Oberammergau.

Some centuries ago, a plague killed vast numbers of people in the south of Germany, and Oberammergau by some miracle was spared.

In gratitude for this, it was vowed that the life of Jesus Christ would be enacted every ten years; and this has gone on for a very very long time. Visitors come from all over the world to experience this remarkable acknowledgement of human gratitude to the Almighty.

In 1960, I was one of these fortunate people through the kindness of Father Franz Mayer and his family.

The whole village takes part, and all the players and musicians are from there. Every visitor is a guest in a local home, and since the whole effort is a deeply sacred one, nothing artificial is used in the Passion play. There are no props, no backdrops and no sound or lighting effects—and no one wears any makeup.
The play commences early morning and ends at sunset. Between scenes of Jesus Christ's life there are tableaux from Old Testament stories; and all of it takes place on a very large stage with the Bavarian hills in the background.

The many hours passed almost too quickly, and I felt a sadness when a glorious Bach chorale ended the performance: but it really was not a performance.
It was the revelation of the life and ministry of Jesus, of his crucifixion and resurrection—all of this intense drama offered with great restraint, as would be expected in the retelling of the most sacred story ever told.

To me, the most moving moments were those of Mary of Magdala, beautiful and with dark ankle-length tresses, and the fine princely man who was Judas.
But this was no surprise; because these two people from the Gospels have always moved me most.

The Grotto of Lourdes on the French-Spanish border is where St. Bernadette is believed to have had her visions of the Virgin Mary, and two very dear English friends, knowing my wish, made it possible for me to visit this beautiful place where miraculous healing experiences amongst others are believed to have taken place, and still do.

It was in many ways an extraordinary experience for me to witness the power of faith that brings people of all religions to Lourdes, which is deeply Roman Catholic, to ask for help and healing.

What a beautiful tribute to the whole Christian world.
I am very grateful to Stephen Rose of the British Foreign Office and his wife Pamela, for Lourdes. They made it possible for me.

Peretz and Yael Gordon were among the first to take charge of the newly established Israeli Legation, later an Embassy, a long time ago in Sri Lanka. They were a charming and bright young couple who worked hard to establish themselves and make friends in the island.

They came to an exhibition of mine at the French Cultural Centre, and
    shortly afterwards I was invited by the government of Israel to teach
    there, beginning with an international seminar of forty-two women, most
    of whom were educated, from twenty-two developing countries, including
    Japan, the Philippines, India, Greece, Yugoslavia, Cyprus, and Africa.

Israel, to a Christian, is the land of Christ. I soon learned it was not thought
    there to be so.

The whole experience was an adventure that was never dull.

The director of the organization that had arranged the long study courses
    had been the commander of the Israeli Women's army, and determination
    breathed in and out of her.

General Minna was tough—very tough—like most of the people I met there at
    that time, for determination in every sphere ordered Israeli life.

I met many interesting people who were very kind and appreciative, and it
    was in their beautiful home in Haifa that I met Professor Jules Kleeberg
    and his wonderful wife Anni, who became two beautiful lifelong friends.

Golda Meir, the Foreign Minister at the time, invited me to dinner and to
    small parties in her very simple home, and the President of Israel and Ms.
    Shazar invited me to their stately and dignified residence.

I was taken one weekend to a Kibbutz, a collective farm, and as we drove in I
    saw an elderly man and his wife wheeling their wheelbarrows full of
    tomatoes.
It was a very hot day, and I said I was sorry the poor old things, sweating and
    red-faced, had to work so hard. Amidst great laughter, I learned that the
    poor old things were Ben Gurion, Israel's Prime Minister, and his wife!

The Hebrew University in Jerusalem wanted to set up a distinguished Faculty
    of Music. With typical shrewd intelligence, Israel invited Jewish and other
    musicians of the world to give at least one concert in Tel Aviv and
    Jerusalem to raise the money for this.

As a guest of the government and as a musician, I was invited to attend a
    series of concerts. My hosts could not have made me happier. And it was
    a revelation to know that many of the world's greatest performers and
    conductors at the time were Jewish.

It was one of the greatest opportunities of my life and I cherish my memories
    of these amazing musicians and their performances.

One evening, a group of musicians sat around a fire near Lake Kinneret, also
    known as the Sea of Galilee. The chief guest was that gracious and
    beautiful violinist, Yehudi Menuhin.

I was introduced to him by the Director of Cultural Affairs and we had a long and interesting conversation.

Pinchaus Zuckerman, Itzhak Perlmann, and the pianist Mindru Katz were at that time little young stars beginning to appear . . .

For argumentative controversial intense people, the Israelis are hard to beat: they are also wonderful in many ways.

* * * *

These two small stories are of two men and two mountains: one is of my father and the nine-thousand-foot mountain Pidru, and the other is of my brother (Mervyn also known as Baba and MJ his initials) and Sri Pada, the beautiful eight-thousand-foot peak, sacred especially to Buddhists.

My father Dunstan, a fearless man, was the first to volunteer to survey the thick jungle lands around Pidru, or Pidurutalalgala, our highest mountain.
Having completed his task with the help of a work force of sixty or seventy men, he decided on something he wished to do before he left.

With a dozen workers he began the perilous climb—something hardly ever attempted before; and after many grueling hours they reached the top, where there were several huge rocks.

Dunstan chose a large rock that seemed to be at the highest spot on Pidru, and his men helped him to scrape it clean of thick lichen and moss. He then took out his tools and chiseled and carved his initials in a bold D M A J on the dark rock.

Then he sat thinking for a while . . .
The men, all Hindus, watched as Dunstan rose and carved two very deep broad lines above his initials—one a vertical line, the other horizontal.

Dunstan had carved on a great rock on the highest mountain of his county, a great deep cross.

And Dunstan was a strong Christian . . .

As he left he placed his hands over the cross, making it his offering.

The workers watched in reverent silence and bowed their heads.

The most beautiful mountain peak in Sri Lanka has many names. It has been called Adam's Peak as the island was known as the Garden of Eden—and Butterfly Mountain, owing to the many million yellow butterflies that fly towards it over several weeks and die in great heaps around it. No one has yet been able to explain this yearly phenomenon in and around May, the month of the Buddha, and many legends have been woven around it. At the summit of this beautiful peak is a footprint, believed to be that of the Buddha from a visit he is known to have made to the island. So the name it deserves is Sri Pada, which means Sacred Footprint.

Hundreds of thousands of Buddhists make the climb as pilgrims to worship the footprint. It is a hazardous and difficult undertaking as the climb must begin at night in order that pilgrims may reach the summit at dawn.

Many years ago, the Prime Minister, Sir John Kotelawala, ordered electric lights to be placed all along the pilgrim route up the mountain, to assist the pilgrims.

It was 1956, and my brother's Australian Director at Radio Ceylon, as our government broadcasting service was called, ordered him to climb the peak and broadcast the first lighting-up ceremony.

My brother tried his best to escape this, but the Director who respected his ability, was adamant.

So he left with a colleague, to perform perhaps the most remarkable duty of his broadcasting career. After a gruelling climb of several hours he reached the summit and was welcomed warmly by the Buddhist priests who have a worship space and a lodging there; and also by the technicians who had awaited him.
All around, and on the pilgrim route was an endless surging crowd of thousands of people.

The ceremony began in the evening.

Having spoken for a little while describing the event, Mervyn waited for the auspicious lighting-up moment.

It happened as the Prime Minister touched the switch.
And Mervyn Jayasuriya gave the news to the entire Buddhist world, in the first broadcast ever from the highest point in the island.

When he had introduced himself to the priests he had told them he was a Roman Catholic. They did not mind.

At the end of the broadcast they blessed him for the splendid effort he had made in the Buddhist cause.

It was strange but true, that the first broadcast from the highest point on the sacred Buddhist peak describing a unique Buddhist ceremony, was not made by a Buddhist, but by a devout Roman Catholic.

My father was an unusual man—a man close to the earth who respected it as I do; and I think he understood me.

My father was my best friend in the very early years of my life. He loved all of Nature too, and loved the sea most of all.

Every morning we would go down to the shore, and as the sun rose the outrigger canoes with their great billowing sails would return from beyond the reef, with their nightly catch.

And every morning the families of the fishermen from the little beach huts would again be the expectant crowd, happy and grateful as all the canoes returned.

School was for me at that stage a strange experience; but then some of my teachers and family thought me strange too—a strange silent dreaming small person. "I cannot understand her," I heard often.

Was this necessary?

Did they not know that a sleeping line can awaken into Dance?

There were three teachers in my small school who I think understood me— the others did not. One was British, the other of Dutch descent, and the third, a South Indian Tamil Christian—Ms. J we called her.

Ms. J was a wonderful teacher who taught beyond the books and opened new roads to knowledge.

When I was eight, she gave me a small book with the title *In Tune with the Infinite*, and seeing my bewildered look she explained that someday I would understand what was written; and she also said, "You will always search Nalini, more than anyone else I know,"

I do: but I have wondered often how she knew or guessed.

My parents who were cousins were both gifted people. My mother who had been taught music and oil painting by a French nun was a good pianist and a skillful painter.

My father and his nine siblings were the choir at St. Paul's Anglican church; all of them, very Westernized, sang played and danced to an old gramophone. (My mother shuddered at the thought of being embraced and fox-trotted at a party. She was after all from Matara, where "proper behaviour," family pride and prejudice remained.)

My father played the violin very well entirely by ear (a gift I also have), and
my parents sometimes played together in our first sitting room, where the
comfortable furniture and my mother's fine Broadwood piano were.

In the next room, was the very beautiful and very uncomfortable antique
ebony furniture, and a long upholstered ebony settee on which I played
the music I heard from my parents.

I was once so absorbed in my performance that I was not aware that my
father was standing behind me watching.

I fled into my room, very embarrassed.

The next morning my father drove out without a word, and two days later a
great lorry brought a huge crate. Inside, was a brand-new shining
Moutrie Bijou piano. The finest the British firm had on display.

I was confused and asked why we needed another piano.

My father explained, "The Broadwood was a gift to your mother from her
father: this Moutrie is my gift to you."

I ran to our back garden and danced and danced among the flowers.
Old Selva, our rickshaw man and his wife watched. With a worried look Selva
confided in his wife that he always felt there was something strange in
this child . . .

The next Saturday, I was taken to Ms. Claribel for my first music lesson.
Dear old Ms. C, soon discovered it was much easier to play the little tune
so I could hear and repeat it, than it was to teach me to read music.
She was a dear person, but a very bad teacher.

All of us enjoyed listening to music. Hymns and songs were among my
father's favourites—the best, "Abide with Me."

He also enjoyed the music of Handel, especially the "Hallelujah Chorus," the
songs of Schubert and the music of Verdi.

My mother played many hymns that we sang together. Her own favourite was
"On the Resurrection Morning." "Londonderry Air," that Mervyn sang
beautifully, and Bach's "Jesu, Joy of Man's Desiring," that his glorious
boy soprano made unforgettable, were also music she enjoyed.

In addition to his favourites Bach, Handel, Schubert and Beethoven, Mervyn,
my brother who was a good dancer, enjoyed the insistent beat, rap and
rhythm of dance music, and he also often sang the Negro spirituals and
the plaintive plantation songs of the African-Americans in his splendid
rich baritone.

At an exhibition in 1997 that the Alliance Française had invited me to have, Mervyn as usual walked round the large hall, seeing nothing, except all the people he would then enjoy chatting with.

That evening, I was very surprised to see him gazing for a long while at one painting of mine.

It was of a tense body leaning, bending fully to the earth—his open palms pressed before him.

It was Christ in Gethsemane asking for his life, but leaving the decision to God.

At Mervyn's request I explained what I was trying to say, and he was visibly moved.

That evening I took the painting home and hid it. The next morning, Mervyn asked about the painting and I told him it was sold. He was very silent and sat thinking.
In January he had his last birthday and *Gethsemane* was his birthday gift. He was speechless . . . Then he wondered how the sold painting was now his. "Who bought it?" he asked. I pointed to myself.

Mervyn had *Gethsemane* reframed, and hung it on a white wall in his bedroom.
He fixed three spotlights, and to look at it is an arresting experience.

Gethsemane was my last gift to Baba, a courageous man and a devout Roman Catholic believer.

I had Mervyn's small book about his experiences over twenty-five years at Radio Ceylon published through the generosity of a wonderful friend, Ana Samarasekera, a devout Buddhist, who would not accept any payment.

The book, full of amusing anecdotes, descriptions and histories of countless people and events also reflects something of Mervyn's colourful personality, his readiness to argue, and to help and fight for any just cause.

Mervyn could not be beaten down easily, nor would he bow to the powerful, and never to the bully.

Canon de Saram, the head of S. Thomas' College, admired "this fellow," as he referred to him, because the great stern man was also just and compassionate.

Mervyn remained defiant and unbowed to the last . . . I did not always agree
with him but I admired his courage. It takes great strength to hold a
different view from the one all the yes people agree with, especially at
work . . . Mervyn had that strength and resolve.

My brother was a very warm and hospitable person. Few could have guessed
that beneath that fun-loving brightly smiling exterior was a vulnerable
and emotional nature. He suffered a deep personal wound in his life that
at first enraged him, and later over the years destroyed his spirit . . .

He did not fight back as he was entitled to, and seldom complained. I think it
was because he believed unreservedly in the justice of God: and he
believed in God's love.

I am proud "this fellow" was my brother . . .

Death and Desolation do not wait for anyone, as the once mighty
Ozymandias, King of Kings, and the confused young ruler of Uruk,
Gilgamesh, discovered.
Death comes, Death takes—and takes unfailingly . . .

My father, my mother and my only sibling, Mervyn, MJ and Baba to my
mother and to me, are all gone into the consecrated earth of the Anglican
part of the General Cemetery in Colombo.

Honoured by friends and family, church dignitaries, members of the
diplomatic corps, officials, the media, and simple rural helpers known
still as servants, they were placed in the earth, draped with flowers and
left in the silence.

All three of my family, strongly Christian, believed in the Christian promise of
Renewal and Return.

I believe this helped them all very greatly.

Our customs and traditional practices at weddings and very importantly at
funerals are preserved. They are from an ancient and abundant past
when people saw meaning in many things.

They had time for reflection: and reflection is a silencing of the mind—a
liberating and refreshing experience that restores . . .

*   *   *   *

I have been asked what the Arts mean to me. They are a tower of mirrors
of numberless complex images.

What one sees is not real—what is real is what the images inspire.

The history of art over thousands of years has been a history of the changing ethos of people, of their beliefs and speculation, their hopes and fears.

Art is a history of ideas that has become a collection of icons, immutable enduring icons celebrating the religious hopes of reconciliation, renewal and return.

Art imitates sublimates and exalts life, freeing the vision from anecdote and offering its radiant peace to all who would receive it.

The rod blooms and the Virgin bears a Son.

Through thirty-three million forms that are only symbols of his energy, the Oneness of the Supreme godhead of Hinduism is established: he is Brahma the sustainer of all the worlds.

Allah and Eternity are celebrated in the unique visual language of calligraphy and abstract decoration.

Islam means submission and the masjid or mosque is the place of prostration.

The Buddha image manifests Buddhist law and cosmological order. Self-absorbed and inwardly smiling in an aloof austere silence, the image relays a spiritual intensity speaking in its silence of the final moment of Samsara or Rebirth when both life and death cease to exist.
This is the ultimate freedom of Buddhist belief.

> *The Hindu affirms Belief*
> *The Buddhist sifts Reality*
> *The Christian confesses Faith*
> *The Muslim proclaims Submission*

And in all is the Presence and Power of the Divine.

"The Lord possessed me in the beginning of my way" (Proverbs 8)

This is the truth within all sacred expression
It is the truth that must be known
and understood

* * * *

I have had the privilege of visiting with the Maoris in New Zealand, the Ainu of Japan, the hill tribe Thais, the Druze in Israel, and Native Americans in the United States.
In their songs and dances, their visual artistic expression, their rituals and tragic remembrances is a power of true spiritual wisdom. It is the vibrant eternal language of the earth and sky, the sun moon and stars . . .

Sound becomes Incantation
Movement become Liturgical Dance
and all Space becomes Sacred Space with God at its center.

Western Christianity proclaimed its faith empowered by a faith without
    alternatives, celebrating in unrivalled eloquence and splendour the life
    and ministry of Jesus Christ.

From the timid yet inescapable catacomb painting of the first Christians to
    the contemporary frenzied or non-art that we now see is the story of
    Christ.

The Byzantine opulence, the restrained and consecrated Romanesque, and
    the supreme Gothic, together with other expressions in between, recall
    and celebrate Jesus Christ in ways that defy even the most exalted
    description.

Christ is also revealed in his pain as he is beguiled, betrayed and outraged.

The story of Jesus Christ is a story without parallel. No single person has
    had a greater influence on human history or nailed a heavier cross on the
    conscience of mankind.

The story of Jesus Christ is a story of power and compassion, of honour and
    deceit, of betrayal and devotion, of Truth and Untruth.

It is a story so unreal that the only way to understand it is to believe
And the world has believed for twenty centuries—because Truth, however,
    unreal, survives . . .

> *They who see me through Form, see me not*
> *They who hear me through Sound, hear me not*
> *But they, who, in the innermost silence of their being know me*
> *Know my Presence everlastingly*

Sri Lanka, Also Called the Garden of Eden

Sri Lanka, that means blessed island, is my country.
Its history is too long, its culture too rich and old, its philosophies and
    religious beliefs too complex, and its beauty too excessive for me to find
    sufficient and adequate words to describe it.

And it is tiny—a dot on the map of the world as it appears to the
    southeastern tip of India: it is alone, this "Pearl of the Indian Ocean," and
    has been coveted and invaded by its great neighbour over the centuries.

According to Marco Polo, it was the most named and the most beautiful
    island in the world—Lanka, Tambapanni, Taprobane, Serendib, Ceilan,
    Ceylon, and finally Sri Lanka.

Apart from the south Indian invaders, we have had the Portuguese, Dutch and British who invaded the island and colonized it. The British were the last, and the longest rulers and had a, certain, affection for this small colony with its docile people—mainly Buddhists.

We have an ancient and recorded history, a beautiful expressive cultural heritage, and an old Indo-Aryan language with a beautiful cursive script that has recorded on hundreds of thousands of palm leaf books the histories of the people, their long royal dynasties, their traditions and beliefs, manners and customs.

The Sinhala, with an Indo-Aryan heritage, are the majority in a mixed population of Tamils and Muslims, Eurasians, Dutch Burghers and the descendants of the Portuguese, Malays and Arabs.

The religions are mainly Buddhism, Hinduism, Christianity and Islam with their various divisions and practices.

The official languages are Sinhala, Tamil and English, with Arabic also used in teaching.

Some of the most beautiful Buddhist temples and monuments still exist, some in excellent condition, and colourful Hindu temples, old churches and mosques are to be found all over the island.
In the old royal capitals are the remains of palaces, once resplendent, telling of royal dynasties of an ancient glory and power.

Sri Lanka surprises greatly.

For such a tiny country to have several fine harbours, and in the northeast the largest and deepest in the whole world is almost too difficult to believe. It is said that in the Second World War, the entire British fleet was housed in this harbour called Trincomalee.

Trincomalee is a prize that many eyes are on.

But we are, since 1948, an independent democratic country, suffering still the wounds and strains of 450 years of Western colonial rule.

At present, the population is 17 million, and the rice-eating population is largely self-supporting.

There are many Buddhist treasures in the island and great celebrations and festivals.

Kandy, in the beautiful central hills, was the last royal capital of Sri Lanka, and in the royal palace of the last king is a very precious Buddhist relic— the tooth of the Buddha, that is taken, in the most spectacular night festival, round the city; and the bearer is a richly caparisoned elephant—

a noble majestic tusker that bears the gold-encased relic on his mighty back, picking his way through tens of thousands of dancers, fire twirlers, drum beaters, flute players, whip crackers and teeming ecstatic millions who throng the city from dawn to cry "*Sadhu,*" as the noble bearer picks his mighty feet like a nimble dancer:
Sadhu invokes Blessing . . .

Sometimes, over one hundred caparisoned elephants walk in the final procession that is preceded by seven smaller processions.

Nowhere else in the world can such a glory of colour, light, and intensity of sacred expression be experienced.

No one can leave untouched by this supreme expression of faithful belief.

A remarkable feature of ancient Sri Lanka is its vast agricultural schemes, devised and built by some of the Sinhala kings, with an expertise that is stupendous.

Experts from the UN who have examined the vast man-made tanks for collecting rainwater to assist rice cultivation, have been amazed at the engineering skills of these royal engineers and builders, of nearly two thousand years ago.

These tanks, one called the Sea of Parakrama, after a king, are in use today, and will be in the future.

I live on one of the most beautiful seashores of the world—a curving, stretch of soft golden sand, with its tall coconut palms, and its great expanse of turquoise water . . . In less than five and a half hours one can drive to the long mountain ranges, passing beautiful waterfalls, rivers and streams.

In every direction is spectacular beauty of earth and water—of animals, birds and butterflies of every colour.

Diverse and magnificent, this may truly be the most beautiful island in the world.

Sri Lanka, famous over centuries for its precious stones had many royal buyers including the Biblical King Solomon who is reported to have bought sapphires, rubies, amethysts and pearls.

We say *Ayu Bowan* as we greet each other; it is Sinhala for "May you live long" . . .
Ayu Bowan, Sri Lanka!

As I look back at my years at Yale where I studied and also had the privilege
of teaching, I believe the most important and enduring influence of
Professor John Wesley Cook's classes, was that I learned a true
understanding of what all sacred expression is—
It is more than Witness and Confession of Faith—
It is Revelation of Truth itself.

In Professor Cook's lectures, quietly and deliberately given, was a deep
Christian faith beneath his vast knowledge . . . He spoke from *within* the
sacred forms he showed, with little of the usual descriptions and exalted
details commonly used in revealing these wonders.

One did not only *see* but *felt* both the words and the images
One did not only hear but understood; that the Reality was within, and the
impulse that created it was blessed.

John Cook's words stayed long after they were spoken because they were
spoken by a believer . . .

I have enjoyed knowing John and Phyllis Cook, and their daughter and son
since they were children: and it was a special Thanksgiving and a special
Christmas for me every year to enjoy these with them in their elegant home.

I have seen beautiful, decorated Christmas trees in many many homes, but
never one as exquisitely beautiful as that in the home of Phyllis and
John. And I was glad to see this quietly sparkling Tree again last year on
Christmas night in this beautiful Christian home . . .

Seeing Christ Again

The Bible has always surprised me. The Old Testament unfailingly so with its
haunting poetry, its ecstatic visions and dreams and its spectacular
stories of events and people.

The Genesis drama of Creation is too pictorial and innocent to be forgotten,
and the commands discourses conversations and exchanges between
Yahweh and His people make the Almighty, not just an integral part of
the sacred landscape but the landscape itself.

There are no narratives as overflowing or vigorous as those in the Old
Testament, and the Almighty has never appeared elsewhere as human as
he does there.

Here is a fierce Warlord, a generous Benefactor when the occasion is right, an
unyielding Judge, and a sympathetic Father to his own children of Israel.

I am always refreshed after I have read the stories of the Old Testament.

They do not retell in Time but are Time itself with the childlike wonder
   sometimes of Becoming.

The Gospels that tell of Jesus Christ, Son of God, born of the Virgin Mary,
   and his three-year ministry are a revelation of the many forces within the
   human being. They tell us more than we know of who we are and who we
   become as we experience Truth and Love without alternatives or
   preferences.

"This is the spirit of Truth . . . He abides in you and He will be with you"
   (John 14:17)

This is a man from the heavens and from the streets—glorified beyond
   understanding and real beyond knowing.

"The most beautiful system of the Sun, Planets and Comets was not to be
   attributed to some blind metaphysical necessity but could only proceed
   from the counsel and dominion of an intelligent and powerful Being who
   governs all things." (Isaac Newton in his *Mathematical Principles of Natural
   Philosophy*)

This Being is Jesus Christ

We had an altar in our home with a red glass lamp that was kept alight.
   Above was a picture of Jesus—a man with brown hair and blue eyes, and
   a large bleeding heart popping out of his chest.

At evening prayers I kept my eyes tightly shut because the altar light made
   the bloodied heart even more red.

Both my parents disliked the picture, but it had been a gift from an old
   Italian priest, a very dear friend, who had blessed it and hung it on the
   wall himself.
And the red glass altar lamp was also from him.
So both of them stayed on, on that long white wall . . .

I have seen Jesus Christ with the faces of the whole world; and as I look
   again at Christ through four painters, I sit for a long while and listen to
   myself . . .

Georges Rouault—Is this a fire of thorns alight upon His brow?
      Moveless, unclaiming, rested in his silence he waits—

            Is he sad?
            Is he angry?
            Is he afraid?
            How can I know
            He says nothing . . .

Mark Rothko—colours escaping—caught again—pressed again into stone: labyrinth of darkness—darkness now darker—

Is this Refusal or Submission?
Knowing or Unknowing?
Is this his dreaming death . . .

(Rothko took his own life)

Rembrandt—In all the robes of might and power you dressed Him—In wisdom grace and immaculate form you fashioned Him . . .

Then in the street where He had once lingered you saw a man—a young street man in simple street clothes—

There was no sea of palms around him, no cheering crowds, no proud little donkey . . .

Which one was He, great master painter?

In Coventry Cathedral in England in boundless space above the high altar He is—silent infinite supreme—

He awaits the world . . .
His dark compelling eyes say again
Come; come unto Me . . .

This is the Christ of Graham Sutherland.
Christ returned to the rebuilt Cathedral after World War II

Jesus returned *to the World*

* * * *

The wisdom of the East, the less is more of Buddhist Zen, and the distilled wisdom of Buddhist philosophy teach ways to silence the anxious mind.

There is a knowing beyond knowledge
It is sanctified
It is simple and pure—
And to people who live very close to the earth, who breathe its vitality and spirit, it is the green shoot rising from the seed, without pain or effort . . .

To the Buddhists this *happens*, as the sky brings both sun and rain, darkness and light; and it is to the unfailing abundant earth that they are grateful.
Buddhism teaches Ahimsa, Non-Violence above all, and this is the most vital aspect of Buddhist life and practice.

Hindus, Christians and Muslims have shared this land for centuries with
the majority who are Buddhist, and each has its particular face and
form.

The Roman Catholics, the largest, and the other Protestant groups believing
in the Divine reality, are sustained and renewed by their beliefs

This land is blessed; and in spite of being relentlessly invaded and robbed it
has never been torn apart. There remains a sense of stability . . . As all
the threatened world hopes, we hope too, that this precious little land
will know both Peace and Blessing always.

Both my parents were from old and respected Southern families from
Matara, a once famous town . . . Both my paternal and maternal
grandfathers held prominent positions under the British, and their sons
(and occasionally their daughters) were educated in the leading
Colombo schools started by the British missionaries.

My paternal grandfather, his wife and children were baptized and practised
as Anglicans, now known as Sri Lankan Christians.

Buddhism is now being returned to its precolonial prominence, but the Sri
Lankan Christians remain strong and faithful

My mother's family, a strong and powerful clan, remained Buddhist, but my
mother at the age of seven, a very intelligent pampered youngest
daughter, charmed by the Bible stories related by her British teacher,
asked her adoring father for permission to become Christian; and it was
not surprising that this fine man, disappointed with certain attitudes of
Buddhist leaders, agreed.

Ada was duly baptized Ada Agnes, and practised her Anglicanism all her
life. However, it would be fair and correct to say there were sometimes
some slight Buddhist overtones surrounding this.

My father, baptized Dunstan Manuel, was a faithful Christian all his life,
serving the Anglican community in every way.

My only sibling, Philip Mervyn, converted to Roman Catholicism when he
was young, and remained a devout believer and worshipper throughout
his life.

A Southern Sinhala family like mine, lives by its strict code of conduct and
an unyielding system of customs and traditions.

Obedience is the cardinal law: and children learn very early in life to obey
and respect their family, all elders, priests and teachers: and a daughter
learns to take second place always, learning to serve with grace and
patience whatever it might cost her.

"Family honour" is religiously preserved, and is applied unfailingly to
women.

The promotion of family status—through "suitable" marriages, always
      arranged by the family, and through job success—was most important
      and still is, amongst our people, whether Tamil, Muslim or Sinhala.

In almost every such marriage endeavour, the marriage broker or *Magul
      Kapuwa* as he is known, is essential. Amongst his duties in finding the
      suitable candidates, are the primary tasks of the dowry, and most
      importantly, of reading and matching the horoscopes.

This takes time, and a few days added here and there adds to the usual fee,
      and then of course the commission the wily fellow collects when the
      adventure that it is, is concluded successfully.

Disasters, if they happen, can always be blamed on the stars and planets. As
      the Kapuwa will explain, these "rulers of our lives" sometimes behave
      very unreasonably.

I have been asked how I would write my Memoirs.

To be honest, at the beginning I did not really know: but I am relating the
      events of my life and the lives of my family as I know them. To do this
      honestly and impersonally is a challenge. Will I skim the surface like the
      little brown sparrow content with the scattered crumbs she finds—or,
      will I, like the resolute gray squirrel, dig the earth to recover his forgotten
      nuts, and perchance his neighbour's?

I do not know, but I will do my best . . .

In this story of people the curtain never falls and the past never disappears,
      but returns walking inwards into itself, echoing and returning a lost
      reality.

I am a musician, and the faultlessly structured returning sound of the Bach
      fugue reappearing in mathematical perfection, is our life; returning
      ceaselessly to hear itself again in other ways.

All of Nature demonstrates this, and Art expresses this reality in many forms.

Return and Renewal undergird the religions of the world with the promise of
      continuity.

And the supreme icon of Hinduism, Shiva Nataraja of Dravidian India, is the
      ultimate expression of the accuracy of Time, and the ceaseless creation
      destruction and recreation of Life.

Shiva Nataraja, in the Tandava Dance, stamps out ignorance the obstacle to
      Wisdom, and dances worlds in and out of existence unceasingly.

My mother had three brothers, and their lives were tragic. One, a brilliant physician, who treated the poor of Matara free of charge, was killed at thirty-six in a road accident. The youngest stole morphine from his brother's surgery and committed suicide when he was twenty-six. The other, Gabriel, Garby to everyone and Unci to me, inherited a vast estate, and was a very able attorney. He was also a champion billiards player, an expert bridge player, a fifty-cigarettes-a-day smoker, an incurable gambler and a hopeless alcoholic.

In a few short years, his offices were shut down, his wealth along with his gambling and drinking companions had disappeared, and the magnificent family home that had been given to him with its ancestral treasures was gone.

Unci, criticized by many, now almost destitute, was my favourite.

He was a tall elegant man with impeccable manners—a true graceful son of a graceful line of ancestors.

"What to do?" we say in Sri Lanka: it was Unci's favourite expression as he dropped his cigarette butt, savoured his last sip of the "old stuff" and bent over his crossword puzzle. (I sneaked in a small quart of his cognac when I could: otherwise he drank a local "old stuff" coconut brew and smoked a cheaper brand of cigarettes.) Always ready to help, never complaining, Unci lived to be a quite healthy seventy-six.

His good friend, a police officer of a well-known Dutch family, who had been sacked from the Force for being drunk on duty, drank alongside Unci into his seventy-eighth year.

I visited Unci every week although my mother had prohibited this, and he enjoyed the small bag of goodies I took him, especially the sweet milk toffee.

One of his large team of helpers from Matara sought and found him after forty odd years. At Unci's funeral, He pushed the gravediggers aside and filled the grave himself. Having grown up in my grandfather's house he had known Unci as a promising and wealthy man . . . He wept for him reduced to penury but was proud that to the end Unci was dignified and graceful even in death.

"What to do?" he seemed to be saying, nodding his splendid silver-white head . . .

There were some house moves until my parents chose Mount Lavinia, a beautiful seaside resort, to build their own house. My brother had been admitted to the best-known boys' school, S. Thomas' College, founded by British missionaries.

Through the years, STC has maintained its high standards of scholarship, sports and discipline. The head, known as the Warden, was always from

Great Britain, and there were many distinguished leaders, until Canon R. S. de Saram, who had a mostly European ancestry, but who was proud to be Sri Lankan, was appointed to the high seat of honour.

The de Sarams are one of our most distinguished families, excelling in many fields, especially in Law, and being some of the finest sportsmen in the country.

We, Jayasuriyas, are several generations of Thomians, and my father a loyal Thomian was delighted Mervyn would be one too.
It is sad he never knew me as a Thomian teacher.

The house designed by my father was near completion and there was great excitement. My father, who was a great gardener, had planned a roof garden and a garden full of exotic coloured flowers and leaves and trees. Several years previous to this, when a good friend who had also been his family doctor, had a rare orchid his wife wished given away, my father was the joyful recipient. But he had been warned that when the orchid bloomed once every seven years, a death took place in the family.

My father laughed heartily, and the great wooden basket was hung in our garden.

Over the years, the orchid began to grow a thick stem from its center of heavy leaves, and now in the course of several weeks the stem over eight feet in length grew great buds from the top to the ground.

That was in September, and we were to move into the beautiful new home on the first of October. My father, after a sudden short illness died in hospital on the twenty-seventh of September . . .

The great buds had opened, and a cascade of purple blue yellow and crimson orchids hung in an amazing glory.
My father never saw the orchid in bloom.

My mother had the cascade cut and placed along the length of his grave. The Death Orchid now was his.

Some days later, she learned of the superstition, and promptly had the orchid taken to the small temple close by. The old Buddhist priest, also from Matara, was a respected friend of my parents.
When my mother related the story to him, the venerable old monk said to her, "My child, for the human being, there are much worse experiences than Death."

The unexpected death of my father, the friend of my childhood, is a wound that never healed, because it was to my very young mind so unjust and undeserved.

But in the heart of darkness is a moment of grace, an almost sacred
compulsion to look further and live on.

Adversity reveals the darkest and weakest side of human nature, changing
friendships, eroding family bonds and unveiling the hard and
unyielding reality of existence.

My mother, baffled by our suddenly changed circumstances, turned for
advice to my father's sister-in-law and her daughter, both wealthy
women and ardent Christians. Being a person of the highest integrity
she did not think anything but the best of their ready offer of help to
manage her financial affairs.

They had a variety of schemes and plans, of investments and business
projects, and a smooth-talking set of lawyers who assured my poor
mother of success and prosperity. Unci had been a brilliant lawyer but
he was hardly ever sober, and there was no one else to advise her.

In a few short years, her considerable wealth had disappeared in all the
projects, which were all either fictitious or bankrupt themselves.

She now faced the grim reality that nearly all her money had gone. Cases in
court followed—more money was spent in legal fees, and nothing at all
was recovered.

At last, this proud unbending daughter of a once-rich family, a widow with
two small children was left almost penniless.

At last, she had to admit she had been robbed.

Her disappointment and rage for a while was terrifying as she sat
motionless in her old chair; and she was weeping.

After some days she had made her decision. She would sell the properties
she had been given; and she did, one by one.

A huge house in the South, in Tangalle, was acquired by the Anglican
Bishop of Colombo, and it became the Anglican school without any
additions to the building.

The years that followed grew more and more difficult. Moneylessness was a
state my mother had not yet grown accustomed to. Now all the
properties were gone, and the hardest decision had to be made.

She had to sell the precious antique jewelry handed down through
generations, and the beautiful jewelry made specially for her.

She sat for many hours looking at these treasures inside the exquisite
ebony and ivory inlaid jewelry box.

Once again, she knew what she had to do: and she did it.

Hardship, bitter as this was, teaches more than you wish to remember, and more than you wish to forget . . . Over a period of time she sold most of her jewelry. When the last set of rubies, her favourite was gone, she sat and wept, almost small and bent with sadness.

My brother and I watched, anxious and afraid. Then suddenly she rose, proud and defiant, with a glint in her nearly blind gray eyes.

We ran to her and held her hands—

This was our mother; and we were proud . . .

Mine was a childhood singular in its power of detachment and its timid aloofness in the midst of the amusements and diversions of childhood.
I was fearful of the fundamental human emotions, and wished for something that could change the tepid predictable existence I knew.

In an Asian family the son has to be educated; and for the daughter, marriage, arranged of course, is the answer.

Mine was a young life that longed to escape—to be free, recklessly free . . . Now I ask are we ever free?

Are we ever free of habit, opinion and doubt? I think I longed for a spiritual freedom that could understand the unanswering reality of death and life—of what was before and is to come—if at all . . .

My early childhood was for me the most wondrous time of all.
Childhood is when everything *keeps becoming*, but *never is* . . .

There were the small daily enchantments of my father's wild garden, where the plants bushes and flower-dripping vines were not disciplined, but grew and blossomed into and over each other.

A tropical garden is incessant colour scent and sound, where jewelled butterflies and golden beetles fly and crawl, and the mynah bird sings his honey-gold song again and again . . .

These colours and sounds, these water diamonds on the blue pond lotus, and the sparkling dew spun grass were my moments of holy wonder.

My early life was full of wonder, as I watched the whole course of Nature, to each beginning ending and return.
I wondered what life really is.

Everyday, the blue lotus in the pond would be there, and every evening it
would sink and disappear in the water. The next morning, another blue
bud would rise and unfold to the sun . . .

As I grew in years but little in maturity, the world became sadly more and
more real—a tedious world often too predictable and very boring.

But I also knew, that beneath the tightly folded sky there were millions of
waiting stars . . .

I found in my somewhat enclosed life a means of escape. Since I was very
young I wrote poems, many of which were published in the youth pages
of the newspapers: but there were some I kept hidden.

One day, for some unknown reason I painted a picture; it was a face of deep
suffering; it was the leper, the starving beggar, the brutalized victim, the
abandoned marginalized condemned person:

I did not know then, but I know now, that it was the Face of Christ . . .

*Now as I read these poems I cannot believe that I wrote them between my
twelfth and fifteenth years. And I cannot believe I painted this Face of
such unutterable sadness.*

Where did these images and words come from?

I do not know . . .

My mother respected our privacy and never searched our rooms, but one
day having lost some important papers she opened my writing table
drawers and discovered the Christ Face, and the sheaf of poems.
She set to work, and when I was seventeen, a collection of poems entitled
Cargo was published by the *Times*, a branch in Colombo of the *London
Times*. David Vast was the publisher.

Cargo was very favourably reviewed by Leslie Cook, a rather well-known
editor of the *British Poetry Broadsheet*.

One fateful dark day, my father's youngest brother Philip, the archaeologist,
visited us with a middle-aged friend of his.

Knowing the precarious financial situation we were in, he had a solution—
this type of solution used to happen quite often, and still does in Asian
countries.

I was to be given in marriage, and this was the very wealthy bridegroom
who would look after everything, and even send Mervyn to England for
his further education that had been my mother's dream.

Discussions followed, preparations were made, gifts flowed in, and formal
visits were made; and I was duly informed of what was expected of me
and what was to follow.

Was I asked, was my consent sought?

(We are in Asia where such niceties do not happen. You are told and you
obey . . .)

Besides, a "luxurious life" was promised. I must have been so shocked that I
did not react at all.

I breathed and moved.

That was all; and the days and nights were one soundless length of Time.

I had one wish. It was to die. I knew I had to, but I did not know how to
bring it about . . .

Then one morning Uncle Bertie my father's younger brother and best friend,
who had heard the news, burst in. He was a favourite cousin and
brother-in-law, and my mother was ready to listen to him.

He knew this man well, and knew he had a family in another country. He
gave details and proof of his report . . . That was sufficient for my very
proper mother. She called Philip, summoned him, expressed her anger
and disgust in no uncertain terms, had all the gifts piled into his car and
ordered him to leave.

Dear dear old uncle Bertie—what a miracle he had brought, and what a
blessed release he had made for me.

I fell at his feet and thanked him.

He was embarrassed. "How could I let you be sacrificed like that?" he said.
"You are Dunstan's precious child." And with that the gentle giant was
gone . . .

Shortly after, an old schoolteacher visited us and offered me a teaching post
in her small school. My mother did not favour the idea, but the financial
situation was becoming perilous.

So I went to teach with a minute salary and a load of work that increased
often. This went on for nearly two years, and one day I had a letter from
Warden de Saram, offering me a teaching post at a very special salary at
St. Thomas' . . .
I was very young, unqualified and very timid. How could I possibly do this?
But it was the miracle I had been waiting for . . .

I thanked God.

I thanked Canon de Saram who had known me since I was four years old,
    and I attended the staff meeting where Canon de Saram announced my
    appointment.
The august body of Thomian teachers welcomed me . . . and I was a
    Thomian teacher.

In the Thomian Blue Black and Blue song we sing, *Esto Perpetua*—"Be Thou
    Forever": and for the fine eight years when I taught some of the nation's
    finest sons, I say again and again, *Esto Perpetua*.

*   *   *   *

I had a wish when I was very young, to be no one and nothing, nowhere, in
    a nounless world.

My mother sometimes regarded me with a puzzled look, wondering perhaps
    how this oddity came about. To be lost is sad, but to be abandoned in
    an uncaring world is a cruel reality; and I often wished the faceless
    world I knew might feel and see; and perhaps shed a tear . . .

One of the most remarkable memories concerns my mother . . . Misfortune
    consumes, but sometimes equalizes and transforms . . .
My brother and I saw an incredible power of endurance and resolve in my
    mother to reclaim a frayed human dignity and return it to a credible
    order of reality.

Would she ask for help? No. Never.

Was this the same person, pampered and dependent, who we all thought
    was helpless?

I recalled the very different ways in which the news of my father's death was
    received by the three of us.

My mother wept silent surprising tears . . .

My brother, a bright happy fellow, fled into his room, hid behind a screen
    and sobbed quietly . . .

And I walked very slowly to my refuge in the Tulip tree and watched the
    flaming glorious sun go down into the wine-dark sea . . .

The years lingered on in tepid uneventfulness . . . Surely there were some
    depths and heights in life, some claim or reward, questions or answers?
    Could life unfold without the experience of any of these?

Mervyn, who had a fine speaking voice, had been chosen by the British expert from the BBC, from a vast number of candidates, for the announcer's post on the Western service of Radio Ceylon, our sole broadcasting service at that time.

He enjoyed his job and flourished.

His was a confident and bright personality; and he later did a splendid job interviewing every important visitor, official, and celebrity who arrived in Sri Lanka.

Many people agreed this was his best work.

Not long after his death, through the great generosity of a friend, Ana Samarasekera, a small book was published about his life before the Radio Ceylon microphone. Mervyn had my father's sharp racy wit, and the book is full of amusing anecdotes, information and history. It has several pictures and reports of heads of state, royalty and VIP's from many countries of the world, and on the cover are two photographs of Earl and Countess Mountbatten being interviewed by Mervyn. He cherished his memory of them.

Life improved in some ways but I continued to work many long hours at S. Thomas' College; then there were music pupils at home every evening except Tuesdays, when I taught Art history at a private school.

The United States had an information center in Colombo, where in a window they exhibited the creative work of promising young people.

I was invited to show some pieces of my sculpture and place some of my poems there. Some weeks after my window show, we had an unexpected visit from a British Council official, Peter Gibbs and his lovely pianist wife, Renee.

My mother and I wondered silently why they had come. After a little polite conversation in which they said they had very much enjoyed my window show at USIS, Peter Gibbs offered me the opportunity of study in London. A stunned silence followed, and to make certain I had not been dreaming, I requested him very politely to say the magic words again.
He did; and I breathed again . . .

I never found out, but I feel Canon de Saram, who knew I had taken the responsibility of a family since I was twelve years old and respected this, may have inspired the British Council offer; and there were others who were interested in my work; Dr. and Mrs. Wade from New Zealand and a couple of British friends.

This was the glorious Spring I had waited for all my life, but I knew I could not go, because my salary at S. Thomas' College would cease, and my music teaching income would not be there. So I let the authorities know I was unable to accept the generous offer made to me.

It was a river of tears when I posted the letter and walked to my STC class.

A couple of days later I was summoned to the Warden's office. This was always a dreaded experience for me.

I entered the room, and the great man looked at me over the rim of his spectacles, and he knew how nervous I was.

After some questions and my faltering answers, I finally told him the real reason for my inability to go.

He seemed very relieved, leaned back, and asked why I had not made this known to him.

To tell him? I would not have dared . . .

Then he said something that I could never have believed possible.
He promised that my full salary would be paid to my mother as long as my study took in London.

I flew out of the room happier than I had ever been in my life; *the Gift had been offered.*

With a gratitude I could not express I thanked God.

All I could call it was *Miracle* . . .

In a few weeks I was on a small Italian ship to Naples, where I would disembark and travel overland through several countries, to see the wonders I had seen in books and dreamed about.

Being ignorant and very eager to see everything possible, I did not realize the hazards and dangers of a young Asian woman traveling alone, and visiting all sorts of places of interest alone.

It is truly miraculous that in all the travel through Italy, Germany, Holland, France and Belgium, I had no real problems and no difficulties anywhere . . . I was free to see, absorb and learn about the art and architecture of the great European cities, and to experience the visual confession of Christian faith, empowered by a faith without alternatives through the Christian centuries.

People ask me which city or country in the Christian world I enjoyed the most—

I have no answer, because each sacred space, each icon, each structure
sound and movement, is a sanctified moment in a sacred history of
Christian belief: each encloses its own moment of holiness . . .

I have known the sacred Presence of Christ recalled a million times through
all the creative forms known to man.

His Presence never leaves: it is there, forever in the believer's heart.

To arrive in London was the moment I had dreamed of, and I was met, and
received later with great kindness by the gracious Ms. Muriel Rose, the
director of my programme of study.

Everything, with customary British efficiency had been arranged.
I was in comfortable lodgings, and I reported at the school after a fortnight of
being taken on a tour of this beautiful historic and noble city of London,
that I had learned about as a small child.

The classes I attended were very interesting and I learned a great deal from
the lecturers.
One of the qualities of the British teacher as far as I know, is that every bit of
instruction is exact and absolute. I certainly felt after all I had been
taught that I knew enough to teach.

History of the visual arts and of music has been one of my chief interests
and a focus of my study. Now, I would have with this new knowledge the
confidence to move on.

The British Council changed my life. I can never forget this.
I was certain this would be my only opportunity to visit these beautiful
historic places, and I did visit them, whenever I had sufficient funds and
time.

On one visit to Paris to good friends, Stephen Rose who was with NATO and
his lovely wife Pamela, I visited the Louvre for hours, an almost
intimidating place like the British Museum.

I enjoy walking. Seeing a city on foot is the best way, and I have done this in
the many years I lived in London, in the years in Paris and Japan, and
on visits to Italy, India and Pakistan.
In the long years in the United States, I have walked the beautiful streets of
Washington D.C., beautiful Connecticut, Louisville, San Francisco and
other cities—and London where I have walked most is a city that has laid
a spell on me . . .

Time moved on, and I knew with deep sadness that I would in a few months
have to return home as I was completing my work and the funding would
soon be over . . .

But another great surprise awaited me. The British Council, pleased no
doubt with my hard work and performance, offered me a two-year
extension to complete work on a degree programme.
Ms. Rose, who I later learned had arranged it, informed me.
I referred this to my mother who told me she needed me back in August of
that year as promised. There were several problems at home, and I had
no option but to return. When I informed Ms. Rose, she wrote me a
kind and beautiful letter, assuring me that if ever I could return the
grant would be available.
I have this letter with me. It is precious.

It reminds me of a gracious lady, and a splendid organization that gave me
my first chance to grow. The British Council does this in several
countries; it helps those who have no means to study abroad; it helps
them to find knowledge that will assist them in their lives.

Some months later I was again on a small Italian ship that would return
me to Colombo. It was peaceful and wonderful to sit alone with the sea
all around me, and to recall all the wondrous sacred places and the
moments of holiness I had known.

As I reflected on the compulsion a believer experiences to leave lasting
witness of his faith, I recognized one great truth.
There is tremendous diversity in the religious expressions of the human
race; people look, feel and speak differently, but they are unified in one
powerful way.
All sacred witness is for all humanity to know that there is in the world a
Power greater than ourselves.

Arnold Toynbee, the great contemporary thinker has said that there is a
Presence in the universe, far greater than man, and man's goal is to
seek communion with the Presence behind the phenomena that
surround him.
The response of people in both East and West to my work never fails to
surprise me: and the opportunities I have been given in several
countries, most of all in the United States, have given me the
confidence to speak somewhat differently about what is known and
familiar: and I have done this through the visual arts and writing.

In my time in school, the Drawing class was what I disliked the most,
because I could not reproduce the wooden objects bottles books and
coconuts before me.

I tried, but they never appeared; so I had to leave the class and spend my
time in the library—a joyful experience for me.

However form and colour always intrigued me.

Through a set of circumstances that assailed me, I began to paint as I felt, and through the years this untutored expression has spoken to many people: and I am deeply grateful.

The Rt. Rev. Dr. Lakdasa de Mel, a cousin of both my parents was the son of one of the wealthiest and most anglicized Anglican families in Sri Lanka.

His father Sir Henry de Mel was heir to great wealth, and his mother, Lady Elsie was a cousin of both my parents.

Bishop Lak, as he was known, went to Oxford University to study law, but after some time he studied and won a degree in Theology.

He was the first local Anglican bishop, and went on to be Metropolitan.

He had two great wishes—one to bring about church union, the other, to assist the Anglican Church in Sri Lanka. At his death all his wealth was bequeathed to the church.

He built the great cathedral of Christ the King in the second diocese he created inland in an old Buddhist town called Kurunegala.
It was with Sinhala architecture, and furniture and effects produced by local artists and crafts people . . .

Bishop Lak was a great sponsor of all our arts and crafts and hoped for a revival of these.

He had baptized me, and was fond of my parents, and he had followed what I had attempted to do; that was to leave the repetitive forms and express Christian beliefs in new ways.

So, he asked me to paint a large mural on the great white wall behind the high altar of his new cathedral.

It was a challenge that had to be met.

I was allowed total freedom to paint the mural as I wished: and I did.
Christ and the Angel Tree was a Nativity never seen before; and Bishop Lak rejoiced; as I understand many of the rural Christians did too.

One question I was asked by a dear puzzled old aunt was, "Where are the animals: I cannot see them."

I told her they were all there; the whole world was there . . .

Some time later, I had an excited call from a Japanese theologian called Dr. Masao Takenaka, a Yale graduate who now taught at Doshisha University in Kyoto. He had seen the mural and wished to meet me. When he and his camera arrived, and especially after our conversation,

I knew this was a serious man pursuing his dream of creating with several others in the Christian world, an awareness of the potential of non-Western Christian expression.

Within a short time, Dr. Takenaka arranged opportunities for me to travel to several countries in the West and East, from Pakistan to New Zealand, to Japan and then to Sweden. It was exhausting and enriching: but the most important thing he did, apart from publishing my book, and arranging lectures seminars and exhibitions for me, was to request Professor Harry Adams to invite me on a research scholarship at Yale.

*   *   *   *

A new programme of study, called Religion and the Arts, had been inaugurated by Professor John Wesley Cook, and on arrival at the Yale Divinity School, I was taken by the gracious Dean Adams to meet Professor Cook.

I was welcomed with great kindness; and the warm goodness of that welcome stayed with me through several years of research and study in degree programmes.

When I left Yale a wonderful farewell was arranged for me. The great hall was full of people, deeply appreciative and kind.

The event announced all over called it "Nalini Day."

It was an unforgettable beautiful tribute from the Religion and Arts Program, directed by Professor Cook, and all my dear friends in this unit; with the blessing of Dean and Mrs. Keck, Associate Dean and Mrs. Adams, and all the Yale people who had so encouraged and enriched my life.

It was Professor Cook's idea that I should work towards a Master's degree. I felt I could not, and told him so.

I recall his words, "Nalini you can and you will"

I worked hard and I did . . .

It is the greatest gift and encouragement to know you are understood and appreciated.

I enjoyed that and still do in this great land.

Elisabeth Luce Moore, the daughter of the famous Luce family in New York, was a remarkable lady. The Presbyterian Church, the YWCA worldwide, several cultural and educational programmes, and people particularly from the East, were sponsored and assisted by her in many ways.

I enjoyed a long weekend with her in her elegant home in Park Avenue in New York.

She gave three dinners in my honour, and I met some very distinguished people, prominent in the arts and sciences; and she took me to her favourite galleries and museums.

It was a truly wonderful experience to have met this great lady, and she wrote to me many times, thanking me for the teaching programmes I did at four universities as Elisabeth Luce Moore Professor.

That was reward enough from such a beautiful and gracious lady.

The Stony Point Centre, about thirty miles from New York, is a beautiful estate gifted to the Presbyterian Church by the Gilmour family of sisters.

Conferences of many kinds, exhibitions, performances and lectures and meetings of people from all over the world have taken place at Stony Point Centre over the years. I have been there many times, and have had the most kind and generous help from James and Louise Palm who were in charge.
It was always a very enjoyable experience, especially to live in the gracious old Gilmour home, to be part of the stimulating courses and the gatherings of interesting people, to hear new voices and ideas.

At the Centre, I sat at breakfast and lunch with Kofi Annan before he became the UN's chief; I met a beautiful singer Elizabeth Hale from the Sioux tribe, an African chieftan, a Maori leader and a regal person who was Cherokee; and many many others on many visits to the Centre.

At an exhibition of my work that stirred great interest, were Dr. Zoltan and Dr. Aurelia Fule who bought a large painting in brown and white of the Nativity—a work of fine rhythmic lines making visual music.

Aurelia and Zoltan became very dear friends: and it was Aurelia's vision and insistence that created a three-year job for me at the Presbyterian Church (USA). It was one of the best experiences I have had.

I am very grateful to the Stony Point Centre and very specially to Jim and Louise, for their generosity and wonderful kindness to me at all times.

Aurelia Fule is exceptional in many ways, and so was dear gentle Zoltan. Aurelia was my colleague, adviser and faithful friend at PCUSA.

My visions and words were used extensively throughout the Presbyterian world and beyond, and I made many friendships with many fine people.

George Telford was the Director of the unit I was in and he and his lovely wife Sally became dear friends.

Then there was that fine young scholar, John Burgess and his wife Deborah, Valerie and Joseph Small, Dick Junkin, Dorothy Adams, Regina Noel and many others in the Unit: and there was my very dear friend Carol Davies and also Jean Cutler—all of them and several others who made my three years in Louisville a joyous and rewarding time.

When I returned home there was a great deal to be done.

My brother had looked after things well, and there were no problems except to revise the daily round; and most of all to have the garden that I love attended to. There were no plans ahead except to prepare work for an exhibition and complete some writing.

Some time later, I visited my very dear friend Anni Kleeberg in Haifa on her ninety-third birthday: and later traveled to the Institute of Sacred Music at Yale where I gave a lecture that evoked a warm response from a large audience.

Joanna Weber had done a fine job arranging everything and also putting up a few paintings I had brought. I was pleased to see Professor John Cook from New York and Dr. Fule and other friends from elsewhere. A short while after, I attended the wedding of Ramesh the son of my best friends Dr. and Ms. Siva of London, to Tesula from India. It was a most lavish ceremony with all the brilliant colour and excitement of Asia. Asians are very generous people, and this warmth and generosity overflowed in what was a true Sri Lankan celebration in London. It was a wonderful experience.

*   *   *   *

The customs and traditions of an Asian family are witnessed most at weddings and funerals—especially at the latter irrespective of the religion of the family. Long white strips of cotton cloth are laid on the path of the funeral procession—this is just one of the customs of Sinhala people.

My father died when my brother and I were very small. I remember how we both held my mother's hands and walked on the white cloth processional path to the Anglican section of the vast General Cemetery.

It was a simple funeral, conducted chiefly by my father's very dear Dutch friend, Rev. Toussaint. Dear old Papa Tous as we called him, was a saintly man, deeply sincere, and deferential when his wife was not around.

He usually rolled his blue eyes at service, announced one hymn number, and
led the singing of a different one. And he did not do otherwise at
funerals; but my father had been one of his best friends and he got
everything right that day.
For years I could not believe what I had witnessed at the cemetery. And I can
still see the long cascade of the Death Orchid on the wet brown earth.

My brother, Philip Mervyn had remarkable gifts some of which he used in his
life.

He had, as a young person, the most beautiful boy soprano voice; later a fine
strong baritone, and an excellent speaking voice.
He had a quick sharp intellect, and a bright personality that made his work
as an interviewer and reporter very successful.

His was a vital cheerful and bright spirit, full of fun and laughter.

Funny stories were something he enjoyed and there were many he related
and wrote about; and a day before he died he asked me for a funny story.

He was one of the first in the life-saving squads trained by Olympic coach,
Harry Nightingale from Australia. He was a fine swimmer, and he was
courageous and fearless as my father was.

Mervyn suffered a deep wounding personal blow in his life, but he hardly
referred to it: nor did he say a word about the very serious illness he
had.
I looked after him to the best of my ability, and he was strong in the
knowledge that I was always there for him.

When I return home this time it will be the first occasion when his great
broad smile and bright "Hi Nalo" will not be there to greet me . . .

It is strange to think that this fine resonant voice that had sounded over the
airwaves of the world will not be heard again . . .

The great house we grew up in is now silent.
No more jokes and funny stories; no more laughter filling the rooms with
brightness . . .

I miss him—Mervyn, MJ to many: Baba to my mother and to me.

My mother's death after four weeks at a nursing home was a very deep shock
to her beloved Baba, and a great sadness for me.

It was like seeing a great strong tree that had withstood powerful storms and
the chopping and slashing of its branches, lean over and fall.

Her funeral had all the customary trappings of a Southern funeral ceremony
and was conducted by the Anglican Bishop of Colombo: and the chief of

the distinguished pallbearers was the Ambassador for the United States, Professor Andrew Corry.

The funeral was memorable for many reasons, because something that had not happened there before took place.

At the end of the Bishop's blessing, the grave workers came together, but Mervyn waved them off; took the two mammoties, held one, and handed the other to me: and he began filling the grave.

I had just cut a clod of earth, but before I could proceed, that great Ambassador Corry took the mammoty from me and began to cut into the soil. He could not proceed either, as someone very politely took the tool from his hand.

Several close friends and relatives shared in the filling of my mother's grave.

It was entirely my brother's idea.
It was his farewell to the great lady he loved, and who loved her Baba more than her own life . . .

I go very occasionally to the cemetery.
The Jacaranda sometimes drops a quilt of purple flowers over all of them . . .
Where are they? I ask
There is no answer

And the purple Jacaranda is blown away into the far corners of the consecrated earth . . .

Firefly Tree

When I was about five, my father planted a young mulberry tree by my bedroom window; but the wondrous flowers I expected on it did not appear.
I asked my father about this and he said "Wait till next year; something wonderful will happen . . ."

A year was almost over, and the mulberry tree was covered with small flowers that grew into sweet red mulberries

I watched and waited
Then one day the tree swarmed with thousands of tiny creatures devouring and growing fat on the mulberries

I have always been very patient; but this waiting was difficult

A few nights later, I awoke suddenly as light filled my room—
I looked and I saw the mulberry tree covered with thousands and thousands of fireflies . . .

Something wonderful had happened . . .
Outside my window was a Firefly Tree planted very specially for me . . .

Confession

Judas – How do I see His Face—
Do I see Him beyond life, beyond death?
In these bloodied hands and feet
This nailed torn remnant of a body
What do I SEE?

I believed when you said you were the Messiah
I believed when you said
You were the Son of God
I believed you were God Himself——
And now
You hang dying?

*   *   *   *

My God
What have I done?

*   *   *   *

How wrong I was
My God
How WRONG——

Confession

Abused vilified
Night's daughter
Hiding from Pharisee rocks ready for her——

But she was renewed; she was blessed . . .

How could Mary of Magdala ever have dreamed
That one day
Her utterance would resound
And the whole world
Would hear her cry
"I HAVE SEEN THE LORD!"

Tributes

Dr. C. Sivagnanam is one of our distinguished physicians who emigrated
    with his talented wife Devi and children in 1974, to England.

In Sri Lanka, he had a Surgery and Nursing Home, and a large circle of
    grateful patients, of whom I was one for many years.

Dr. Siva, as he is known, has practised with his great professional skills
    and devotion in London, treating 6,000 patients.

In recognition of this remarkable physician's splendid service, Dr. Siva was
    honoured with "The Citizen's Award" by Prime Minister John Major, in
    1994.

Dr. Siva continues to serve the British public as Medical Adviser at
    Greenwich Hospital in London.

When I first met Devi, the glamorous wife of Dr. Siva, I was struck by her
    northern beauty and grace, and most of all by her warmth.

The lively daughter of a wealthy family of several doctors and now resident
    in London, Devi decided to pursue her great interest in cosmetics and
    fashion, particularly for women of colour.

She set to work, studied, gained the experience she required, graduated,
    and developed into the expert she is today, as the UK Manager for the
    well-known cosmetics business known worldwide, as Fashion Fair.

With her sharp intellect, her great organizational skills, her courage, and
    her unfailing loyalty, she is an example to Asian women, to dare and to
    do—and to achieve great success.

Devi has been the most caring faithful friend—
I am strong in the knowledge that she and Doc have been and always will
    be there for me . . .

Seldom now in her gorgeous silk saris, she is today the top executive, chic,
    yet glamorous in her business suit.

I have many, many friends in many countries—wonderful caring friends—
    students, colleagues, teachers, comrades, and benefactors without
    whose abiding interest and assistance I could not have moved on in life.

They are too, too many for me to name in these pages; but never too many
    for me to recall with deep gratitude.

Ruth and Michael Thornton were my first friends, and in the years when
    Mike was Director of the Overseas College, housed in the ancient

English castle in Farnham, I enjoyed visiting them there, and later in Guildford.

They once commissioned me to paint a very large hanging for the old Refectory in the Castle.

It is of a gathering of tenth-century British nobles and church dignitaries at a royal feast, and was beautifully mounted and hung by Ruth.

I understand it is greatly admired, and until visitors read the fine plaque is believed to be the work of a Britisher!

When the High Commissioner and Ms. James George of Canada, and High Commissioner and Ms. Gundevia of India, were leaving their posts in Sri Lanka, both of them held exhibitions of my sculpture stained glass and paintings at Canada House and at India House: on both occasions banquets followed.

I was honoured and very grateful to them both, for this beautiful gesture of their appreciation and friendship.

The French Ambassador M. Jean Brionval was a most interesting and lively person.

Sri Lanka was his last post, and his charm won him many friends in my country.

He visited us occasionally, stayed long, and enjoyed conversing with my mother, who remembered a little school French, and was glad to use it haltingly.

André Malraux, the French Cultural Minister, and an authority on Art and Architecture, was on a voyage soon after a tragedy in his family: and he stopped in Colombo to see his old friend M. Brionval.

Ambassador Brionval had a private dinner for the great man, to which M. Malraux's friends, the envoy for Italy and his wife, then in Colombo, and I, of all people were invited.

M. Malraux talked incessantly, addressing me often as I sat by him; and I nodded approvingly. He seemed very pleased; but since all the conversation was in mostly rapid French, I had no idea what it was all about . . .
Did I enlighten him? No. How could I?
To my great surprise I was invited later that year to Paris to exhibit my work; and the French Ministry of Cultural Affairs acquired one of my paintings.

Dear Ambassador Brionval: it was sad to see him go . . . And he supervised
the packing of the four paintings, and the large clay incised pot he had
bought from me.

He was a rare person.

Apart from all these wonderful friends, there were all the institutions and
organizations in several Western countries and Japan that appreciated
my work, and created ways for me of deeper knowledge and
understanding.

There is no way I can either understand or account for these, except by
thanking God again for the Miracles He has ordered in my life . . .

Lines from Poems in *Cargo*, a Book of My Poems
Published by the *Times*

We spend ourselves
On a gathering of painted shadows
Painted and set up to gauge our talent:
We spend our breath and our art
Striving to get
Between the shadow and paint
                                            At 13 years

You are the finished dream and the dream to
        be:

Unmoving, unread
You are the shadow in the water
And I cannot gather you with my hand . . .
                                            At 13 years

I must arise and spill my colour in the world
Or from long use my soul will grow
Dull and prosaic as my wooden desk
And my thin lead pencil . . .

I must arise and stretch my bended knees in
        the living grass

I must go
Into the unhindered land . . .
                                            At 13 years

The worms are where the violin used to be
And the song has become
A part of the eternal air . . .

                                    At 13 years

He speaks
But the world pulls its head down puzzled
It knows not nor understands . . .
Quietly now he stands on the silent mountain,
        rapt unseeing
And from the world that knows him not he
        goes
Quietly
Taking his song with him
Down the un-echoing ages . . .

                                    At 13 years

Now comes the daylight clamouring to a close
Where falls the earliest dew upon the sleeping
        rose:
Beneath the tumbling hills the hour of rest
Falls through the closing valleys
And the West
Accepts the dying sun

                                    At 12 years

The thoughts of you are long thoughts
Over hills and rivers running
Caught into winds
Adrift with stars
And singing . . .

                                    At 14 years

After ponderous thoughts
A little nonsense . . . (not really, because it is about some folks I enjoy)

(My father, mother and Mervyn would agree a little nonsense is good for us)

I love turtles:

The turtle is wise
He is gentle ingenuous
Peaceful, serene

Like his cousins
He carries his own house
So he is never a trespasser squatter or
        invader

When his wife is annoyed with him
He retreats into his house
And no one, not even she can even telephone
        him

When his neighbours are quarrelsome
He stays well inside his house for hours
And when he appears
He appears one foot at a time . . .

The turtle
Lives hundreds of years (so they say)
And he lives hundreds of years
Because (like me)
He is vegetarian . . .

The turtle is known to weep
(especially now in SL
where killing is a contest)

the turtle
swims walks paddles along—
and they say he dreams of flying . . .

he walks slowly
on the sea sand
wouldn't you
if you had to carry your house?

I love the turtle because he is not a politician
Because
He is such a decent polite person
Minding his business, doing his turtlish
        duties
And looking after
His several hundreds of turtlits . . .

I love the turtle
Because
He is so artless benign tractable . . .

If I had a choice
I would like to be a turtle . . .
Perhaps I can ask him
What my chances are
When he comes next full moon night
To the Mount Lavinia beach . . .

(let me know
if any of you all
may also
be interested)   N.

Wind has voices, Rain has voices—voices I know
    and understand—
Now the Silence, unclaiming, holds me in its spell . . .

I watch the sea wrapping and unwrapping its endless
sun braided shawl around my island home . . .
The last seagull has left the sky
And I wait alone . . .

                    *   *   *   *

Dreaming remembrance unwraps memory, walking
Inwards into itself; unfolding a quilt of stars to cover
    the night . . .

As the darkness wraps my seashore I watch . . .
The darkness threads a thousand stars . . . no
    darkness
Is left in darkness but is transformed into stars . . .

In this Silence, too deep to understand except within
the silence itself, rested now, I look at my hands—
Worn empty silent hands—
Where is the power that once spun me round the
    Sun?

And where are all the years, where have they gone?
Have they gone back into me like the sunset that will
    return in light? . . .

Rebirth Resurrection Renewal—the promised certainty
Of Return . . . a new adventure, a chastening
    experience,
a sanctified beginning . . .
Who knows?

Or, like the Asian *Pratima*, the Incandescence from
The Sacred Image, beyond itself: unceasing

The Sea is full of metaphors
I have watched the might of the swelling wave rise
To the sky, crash, and dissolve into foam . . .

This is the story of all life . . .

I follow the blazing evening sun as it sinks into the
     wine dark sea
I know it will return:

And the spent wave will rise again to the sky . . .

* * * *

Remembering with gratitude for all we have received is both necessary and renewing, and I now offer my deep gratitude to my parents, my brother, a few caring relatives, to my teachers and my friends at home, and all over the world; and to the various institutions and countries that have helped me to walk new ways of Wonder and Understanding.

Chief amongst these have been the United States, the United Kingdom, Germany, France, Japan, the Philippines, and Israel.

My friends in Germany, Professor H. G. von Stockhausen and his wife Margret, have enriched my life in many wondrous ways, and Dr. Finn and Lene Hjalsted of Denmark have been rare beautiful friends.

Also, Dr. Yoshiko Ishikki and Professor Masao Takenaka, both of whom translated and published my books, Sr. Dr. Bellarmine Bernas, and my Dutch music teacher Eleanor Beling who have all lighted my life.

Then a host of young and old friends, Wim and Sheila, Mark Bostock, Margot de Alwis, Anne Gibson, Chloe and Cecil, Sam and Mukta, Lalith and Sicille, Shirlene and Rocky, Deen, Hamza, Shafee and Oli, Sophie, Jacky, Annick and Simone from France, Ilse and Elsa from Germany, George and Sally, Nihal de Lanerolle, Frances McFall and Inge Lueders from the United States; Suhada, Nilantha, Merton and Lalani, Chira and Ashi, Duncan, Noel and Hyacinth, Dr. Douglas Arndt and Cedric Jansz. There were many from the diplomatic corps who helped me and chief amongst these were Ambassadors David and Pauleen Aiers, James and Carol George, and Margaret Catley Carlsson, and German ambassador Dr. Schworbel and Dr. Ms. Schworbel.

I must pay a special tribute to the United Board for Christian Higher Education in Asia in New York and its great president, Dr. Paul Lauby, for the wondrous help *always* given to me in my years in the United States.

Before I left Yale, I painted a triptych of Jesus between his own disciples, Peter and Judas, who, we are told, denied and betrayed him.

Professor Keck, with beautiful words, dedicated the triptych for use in the Marquand Chapel, and Thomas Murray played the *The Swan of Tuonela* at my request—the last evening of the dying swan.

After the service, a large gathering assembled in the Great Hall for a reception, some speeches, and slices from the huge cake in honor of "Nalini."

Nalini Day, from the Religion and Arts Program at Yale, remains a sacred memory; and it is sacred because it was blessed by such kindness and love.

What goodness and grace were mine.

I thanked God.

Now as I near the end of these memoirs, I must express my very grateful thanks for my time at the Overseas Ministries Study Center, for the deep concern and kindness shown to me by everyone, and for the appreciation expressed with great sincerity and warmth for whatever I tried to do.

OMSC was a very new experience for me, seeing, meeting and hearing people from all over the world, trying to understand them and relate to them even a little, because my association with the residents, visiting faculty and foreign visitors was very slight.

I had my own programme of work that I had to accomplish; but there was every assistance available if I ever needed it.

There is a quiet efficiency here, and a gracious kindness extended to all who come to OMSC to study, for renewal and deeper understanding for their work in their chosen or assigned places all over the world.

The executive director, Jonathan Bonk, and his lovely wife, Jean, are kind and caring people, gracious attentive and supportive.

In my humble opinion both of them have a very full understanding of what Christianity implies and involves—I am honoured and enriched by their friendship and I ask that the Presence of God will illumine their days.

Jeanne Dilg, has been a very good friend, caring and supportive: and everyone else, in the offices, the apartments and grounds of this fine institution have always been ready to help me.

I shall be sad to leave this place where OMSC has been a family to me.

I thank you all, and ask for all God's care and blessing to be yours, always.

Ayu Bowan, as we say in my language, Sinhala, or May you live long!
Ayu Bowan, OMSC.

*   *   *   *

> *When the Sun rises*
> *Life is alight again . . .*

In our world, now emphatically divided into colours, the East and its expression may appear even more perplexing and remote than before.

The resolute line of Western thought becomes cyclic movement in the East, where Suggestion and Reflection are important; and where Conclusion is seldom met.

The expression of sacred ideas in all religions is a power and a wonder beyond knowing, and it happens when renewed vision replaces what is trite and exhausted.

For many years, I have known a professional experience of Hindu, Buddhist and Islamic sacred art and architecture: and I have known the transcendent Art and Architecture of the Christian World that has held its believers in a realm of awe . . .

There is no sorrow as deep and no radiance as enduring as the sorrow and splendour of the Story of Jesus Christ.

And nothing can exceed the spiritual power and diversity of the Confession of Christian Faith.

We are one, in this world of remorseless reminding Time,
Hoping, believing in renewal and continuity—
We belong in the internal exile of Judas Iscariot—
We belong with the rapture of Mary of Magdala—
With the bloodied footprints of martyrs
And the dance of angels
We belong together . . .

We are one
As we lose and find ourselves . . .

Who knows
There may be above us
The Star of the Magi . . .